"Every woman who has a spiritual thirs[...] read Amy Nappa's heartfelt book. *Thirs[...]* and powerful. Don't miss out on this thirst-quenching read."

"Drink deeply of this beautiful book. In *Thirsty*, Amy Nappa taps into every woman's longing for someone to truly see, understand, and love us. Just as Jesus did for the woman at the well, he comes to each one of us, peers into our fears and failures and parched souls, and invites us to drink deeply of his love, grace, and life. If we're honest, we're all at that well — desperate to encounter the One who can finally and fully satisfy our deepest thirst. Amy's inspiring book reminds us that he's there, waiting for us. And aren't we all thirsty for more of him?"

thirsty

Meeting Jesus at Your Deepest Need

AMY NAPPA

NAVPRESS®

NAVPRESS⬤

NavPress is the publishing ministry of The Navigators, an international Christian organization and leader in personal spiritual development. NavPress is committed to helping people grow spiritually and enjoy lives of meaning and hope through personal and group resources that are biblically rooted, culturally relevant, and highly practical.

For a free catalog go to www.NavPress.com
or call 1.800.366.7788 in the United States or 1.800.839.4769 in Canada.

The Navigators is an international Christian organization. Our mission is to advance the gospel of Jesus and His kingdom into the nations through spiritual generations of laborers living and discipling among the lost. We see a vital movement of the gospel, fueled by prevailing prayer, flowing freely through relational networks and out into the nations where workers for the kingdom are next door to everywhere.

NavPress is the publishing ministry of The Navigators. The mission of NavPress is to reach, disciple, and equip people to know Christ and make Him known by publishing life-related materials that are biblically rooted and culturally relevant. Our vision is to stimulate spiritual transformation through every product we publish.

ISBN-13: 978-1-60006-093-9
ISBN-10: 1-60006-093-5

Cover design by Jason Gabbert
Cover image by Dover

Some of the anecdotal illustrations in this book are true to life and are included with the permission of the persons involved. All other illustrations are composites of real situations, and any resemblance to people living or dead is coincidental.

Unless otherwise identified, all Scripture quotations in this publication are taken from the HOLY BIBLE: NEW INTERNATIONAL VERSION® (NIV®). Copyright © 1973, 1978, 1984 by International Bible Society. Used by permission of Zondervan Publishing House. All rights reserved. Other versions used include: *The Holy Bible, New Century Version* copyright © 1987, 1988, 1991 by Word Publishing, Dallas, Texas 75039. Used by permission; the *Holy Bible, New Living Translation* (NLT), copyright © 1996, 2004. Used by permission of Tyndale House Publishers, Inc., Carol Stream, Illinois 60188. All rights reserved; and the *King James Version* (KJV).

Library of Congress Cataloging-in-Publication Data

Nappa, Amy, 1963-
  Thirsty : meeting Jesus at your deepest need / Amy Nappa.
    p. cm.
  Includes bibliographical references.
  ISBN-13: 978-1-60006-093-9
  ISBN-10: 1-60006-093-5
  1. Bible. N.T. John IV, 4-42--Criticism, interpretation, etc. 2. Samaritan woman (Biblical figure) 3. Christian women--Religious life.
I. Title.
  BS2615.52.N37 2008
  226'.506--dc22
                        2008014827

Printed in the United States of America

1 2 3 4 5 6 7 8 / 12 11 10 09 08

For Joani Schultz, who is always thirsty for Jesus . . . and a tall glass of iced tea.

As the deer longs for streams of water,
so I long for you, O God.
I thirst for God, the living God.

— Psalm 42:1-2, NLT

Let anyone who is thirsty come to me and drink.

— John 7:37, NCV

contents

foreword

Have you ever felt so overwhelmed with life that you just didn't think you could even get out of bed? And the thought of work — any kind of work — just made you sick to your stomach? I think that's where I was this morning, just knowing how full my plate was. But somehow I managed to crawl out of bed, put on my robe, turn on the coffeepot, and settle in to this new book, *Thirsty: Water for a Woman's Soul.*

I thought perhaps I'd spend a handful of minutes quickly passing through the pages, getting to the point and then moving on to my next task of the day. But I must tell you, Amy Nappa had me at "intro." (smiling)

I could not put this book down, because I didn't want to miss anything. I am that Woman at the Well. I am broken and thirsty. I have been deeply wounded. I've been betrayed and disrespected. I have felt abandoned and afraid. I desperately want to know God's promises for my life and to take him at his word.

As I dug into this book, I wept reading each word, feeling the presence of God in my life at this exact moment and knowing he's waiting patiently for me with each new season of my life — even here in my study today. What a sweet reminder of his constant, deep, pursuing love for me — and what an unexpected place for me today to feel this. But that's Jesus. So unexpected. So surprising. And once again he knew exactly where to find me, he knew all about it, and he knew just what my soul needed.

I have questions. I have doubts. I have walked through grief and sorrow after the tragic death of my husband over six years ago. So I know our God is a God of mystery, that's for sure. I think many of us often find ourselves asking God, "Why?" That is such a normal question to ask, and I'm not sure we'll ever have the full answers this side of heaven, but one thing I know: Just as the Woman at the Well discovered long ago, you will always see beautiful glimpses of Jesus in everything if you just look for him. And I think it's in those moments when we know we are not alone that God is very real.

He longs for us to be free. He longs for us to walk in truth. He wants us to know pure joy and to rest in his peace when nothing makes sense. Ask the questions. Seek and find for yourself. It's in these times that I believe our faith is truly strengthened. Not because we have all the answers now, but merely because we begin to trust in the God that we've come to know intimately, and trust that he knows exactly what he's doing. Remember, Jesus knows every detail of your life before and after it happens, just like he did the Woman at the Well, and he will not leave you high and dry. There is living water for all through the promises of God. And in that comes great healing.

I can close my eyes and see a picture of Jesus. He had waited for me to wake up all morning, knowing what my soul needs. He couldn't wait to talk to me about my life through these pages — and remind me that I am an overcomer. That my life is evolving into something beautiful. I'm not there yet, but I'm on my way. We are all on our way.

May we always be thirsty for the things of God and follow after his heart. When we do that, we drink from pure living water. Eternal life. Now that's a promise!

Thirsty, anyone?

> — *Tammy Trent, recording artist, author, and speaker*

acknowledgments

Grateful thanks go out to many people for their support and contributions to this book.

First, to my husband (and literary agent!) Mike Nappa: Without you, it would never have been written.

Thanks very much to Tammy Trent, a woman whom I admire personally and enjoy professionally as well. Your music and your life speak volumes to women everywhere, and I'm grateful you were willing to take the time to write the foreword to this book. You are a blessing!

Thanks also to Dan Benson and Rebekah Guzman at NavPress. You two saw the potential in this manuscript long before anyone else did, and I appreciate your support. And to my editor, Jamie Chavez, your skill and insight simply made this a better book.

Last but not least, I would like to gratefully acknowledge the authors of the reference works I've listed in the bibliography, whose valuable information I hungrily soaked up and occasionally used during the research and writing of this book.

a little prince

Water may also be good for the heart.

— *The Little Prince*

He inhales deeply, tasting the heat, the sand, the desperation in his every breath. Eight days ago his plane crash-landed in this arid, barren place. He should be glad to be alive; instead the vastness of this empty, endless desert simply reminds him how hopeless — and fleeting — his life really is.

The warm dryness of the air scratches against the back of his throat. The last, precious dampness of his water supply has finally run dry, and one thought now dominates his consciousness:

I am about to die of thirst . . .

I know this anonymous pilot is really only a fiction, that he's merely the literary equivalent of a self-portrait by Antoine de Saint-Exupéry, brought to life in the beautiful, classic story *The Little Prince*.[1] But right now he is as real to me as my own breath, as vivid as my own existence. And so we walk together, this unnamed pilot and I, shipwrecked together in a desert of the imagination. And I think to myself, *I, too, have known something of thirst . . .*

We stare at the unblinking horizon and absently lick the cracking skin that covers our lips, vaguely aware that it hurts to do so, mildly aware of the tiny, bleeding cuts that crisscross those same lips. Eight days, and we still can't find a way to repair our plane, to climb into its sanctuary and fly away to the heavens where life and family and friends — and yes, water — await us. We wonder if anyone out there in the hidden reaches of the world is thinking of us, worried about us while they sip with careless disregard a tall glass of water chilled with ice. And again, we can't escape the truth:

We are about to die of thirst.

And so we walk, feeling the sand groan and swim beneath our leaden feet as we step, one foot after another, into the vast glittering stillness of nowhere. We must find a well . . . but the desert is as big as the sky. We feel the fever of thirst and begin to wonder if we are really in a dream. When night falls and the moon and stars come out, it feels as though we've been walking forever. We are tempted simply to lie down and die. But still we trudge forward, not knowing where we are or where we are going. The memory of water drives us on.

We are not alone in this parched, lonely place. Beside us walks a boy.

It's absurd that this child should be here. He appeared as if from nowhere on the first night of our desolation, claiming to come from the heavens, unafraid — or unaware — of the silent danger that surrounds us. He has no name, but he faces the Sahara with unshakable nobility, like a prince surveying his father's kingdom. So that's what we have taken to calling him: the Little Prince.

"What makes the desert beautiful," our Little Prince says suddenly, "is that somewhere it hides a well."

And within the delirium of thirst, a new emotion seeps in. Astonishment. He is right, this boy, this Little Prince. "The stars, the desert," we say to the child, "what gives them their beauty is something that is invisible." And we all long for — hunger and thirst for — that invisible cistern that holds the power of life.

We pause to rest. Our tongues feel swollen and useless. Our nostrils are clogged with dust and heat. Our skin is red and stung by a thousand pinpricks left by the sun. It would be so easy simply to die. To die of thirst. But thirst does not kill; absence of water does that. Thirst drives us to remember, to live — and to seek life-giving water.

The boy beside us is sleeping now, and our Little Prince seems for the first time to truly be a small, fragile child lost in a desert.

Our bodies want to die, but our thirst and the boy sleeping beside us won't allow it. Carefully, achingly, we draw him up into our arms. And we walk.

The desert never ends. But still we walk.

The night begins to fade.

And we walk.

Our chests throb. Our minds wander. Our throats grind to dust. Our muscles cramp and complain.

We walk.

And in the morning, at the first break of day,

we find the well . . .

It is at this point that I close de Saint-Exupéry's book, leaving my unnamed pilot alone with his prince to drink deeply from the well they have found. And as I reflect on their experience, I remember again what first drew me to them.

I, too, have known something of thirst.

You see, my soul often feels as though it has crash-landed in a desert, into the physical existence of a human life. Into the place where my spirit feels bounded about by the endless Sahara of temporary things — of material possessions, of comfortable homes, of grocery lists and carpools and corporate ladders and glass ceilings and difficult marriages and heartbreaking losses and chronic illnesses and so much more. Within this arid, soul-parching existence, my spirit often longs for — *thirsts* for — something more.

For more than my eyes can see.

For something invisible.

For Life with a capital L.

For rivers of living water to flow through my soul.

Like the anonymous pilot of de Saint-Exupéry's story, I also walk through this desert with a companion. He is not a Little Prince, but is instead the Prince of Peace. The King of kings. The Son of God himself.

And in my life's desert it is not I who carries him, but Jesus who carries me. Together we walk across the sun-scarred troubles of my life, across my frequent failures and mistakes, over the dunes of my selfishness and sinfulness, beyond the broken rubble of my plane-wrecked relationships and foolish decisions. And he never tires of holding me up, of taking me just one step farther.

"I am about to die of thirst," I whisper to him often. Too many times.

Yet every time I think I'm finished, that I'm done for, that this desert life has finally won its victory over me, I taste something cool and wet and soothing in my soul. I feel his Holy Spirit washing over me, filling, quenching, strengthening, bringing health and nourishment to the thirsty longings that parch my inmost being.

My Prince has found for me a well of living water.

He has brought me back to life again.

Dear friend, I am guessing that you, too, know something of thirst. That you, too, have taken a good hard look at your life and found it wanting. That, on occasion, you've said to yourself:

There must be something more.

Take heart, my friend. You and are I not alone in this desert experience. We are only two of many, many women whose souls have also been thirsty. And we can find that well of living water we so desperately desire. Do you know how I know this is true? Because another woman told me so — showed me so. I don't know her name either, but I met her once, in the pages of John's gospel. History knows her only as the Woman at the Well.

You and I, however, shall meet her again as someone like you and me, as just a woman.

A thirsty woman.

Let's go meet her right now.

waiting

Now he had to go through Samaria. So he came to a town in
Samaria called Sychar. . . . Jacob's well was there, and Jesus,
tired as he was from the journey, sat down by the well.

— JOHN 4:4-6

It was the waiting she hated the most.

*She could deal with the hateful stares. She could close her ears
to the self-righteous insults whispered behind her back. She could
even turn away from the mean-spirited moments that punctuated
her relationship with the Man. That's what she'd taken to calling
her lover lately. The Man. It seemed fitting, after all. He was just one
more in a long line of leavers. But every woman in this Samaritan
village of Sychar needed a man. A protector. A provider. An occa-
sional bestower of affection. And so she stayed. And waited.*

*He left early in the mornings, off to work in the barley fields to
earn their living, to keep food on their table. As was her womanly
duty, she rose early with him, made him breakfast, wrapped a meal
for him to eat for lunch. It was the woman's responsibility to collect*

water each day as well. But when the Man was gone and the rest of the village women went to fill their jars from Jacob's well on the outskirts of town, she sat in her tiny living quarters and waited. She could hear them passing by, gossiping and laughing on their way to the well. They had been her friends once, at least some of them. She had laughed and chattered right along with them. It was the way of the women in this community, sharing the burden, lightening the load with friendship and family. But she had long forsaken that benefit of life.

It wouldn't do to socialize with those people. Not now. She would not be welcome.

Oh sure, they'd take her money when she traded it for supplies at the market. And they'd bring her washing or little jobs to do if one of them got sick or injured. They would use her as they needed. They would even allow her a place in the temple from time to time, as long as she was with the Man and didn't distract the other women's husbands and sons. But they wouldn't befriend her. They wouldn't join with her in turning the chore of fetching water into a joy of seeing friends.

Not now at least. Not after five husbands. Not after she'd become concubine to a sixth man — to the Man. In this village, where religion ruled all, her moral failings had branded her an immoral woman long ago. And that meant she was an unwelcome participant in this little community. In fact, had the Man not taken some semblance of pity on her, she very well could have starved in the streets as her former friends abandoned her.

So they went to Jacob's well, coming and going as the morning progressed. And she waited, keeping herself busy as best she could — milling grain, baking bread, sweeping and cleaning, and whatever else needed to be done — until the sun had risen high overhead and the heat of the day drove most other women indoors. Until the others were sure to be long gone. Until it was safe to go to the well alone, and unnoticed.

But she hated the waiting of the day. It gave her too much time to think. To remember. To hate the woman she'd become, living the life she'd never expected to live. And then finally, thankfully, it was time.

She gathered her jar, covered her head to protect herself from the midday sun, and went out into the world. She walked with the confidence of a comfortable outcast. Her feet traveled the distance without causing her mind to think much about it; she'd made this trip a thousand times. Mentally, she began making a list of the chores to be done once she got back with water in her jar. She could feel the sun's warmth on her skin — a good feeling. And she swallowed a gulp of dry air. Perhaps she would linger at the well today, taking a leisurely moment to satisfy the morning's thirst before attacking the day's chores still left before her.

Yes, she was thirsty.

As she neared the clearing where Jacob's well had stood sentinel for centuries, she pulled up short.

There, on the short wall that circled the well, a man sat in the meager shade of midday.

He was waiting.

Did she know, I wonder?

Did the Woman at the Well have any warning at all that the man sitting beside the well that day would radically change the core of her very being? That she would never be the same, that the world would never be the same, after an all-too-brief meeting with the one and only Son of God?

I think it would be cool if life were sometimes more like the movies, if — just at the key moment when something significant is about to happen — life would linger like a camera on a potent scene or object or face. The world would slow down, just a bit, just long enough for us to know, to think, *Hey, something important is about to happen. I'd better pay attention!* A light thumping sound, like a previously unheard heartbeat throbbing in the ears, would fill unseen surround-sound speakers. The background music would heighten almost imperceptibly, and involuntarily we would catch our breath in our throats. Then, just as quickly as it came, that slow-motion moment would rush away in the wave of oncoming events, and the world would proceed as normal.

But we'd *know.*

We'd know something special, something unique, something eternal was peeking through the cracks of our lives.

God doesn't always work like Hollywood, however. Sometimes (okay, often) he arrives unannounced into the mundane moments, blending the divine and the ordinary with such effortlessness that we can't help but be awed by it afterward.

I think this is what happened on that historic day when Jesus Christ met a Samaritan woman by Jacob's well in the ancient Middle East. Our heroine, the woman in this story, thought it was just another day, a period of pale sunshine that punctuated the hours between her darkened nights. She was thirsty; she needed to fetch water for her physical body, to keep it healthy and hydrated. But hidden beneath that physical need was a deeper thirst in her heart, a spiritual longing for meaning, for unconditional love, for eternity.

It was this thirst that Jesus came to satisfy . . . and she was caught totally unaware by his presence.

Why did God choose that day, and that place, to open the floodgates of heaven and pour out his love into her soul? To let her go thirsty through so many years of heartbreak and husbands and debasement before her community of peers? I honestly don't know. Who knows why God does anything, really? But I do know this: He came. And when she wasn't there, he waited patiently for her until her own need drove her straight to his presence. And he met her, of all places, by the side of an ancient, dirty, much-used, mundane, grimy well. Let's explore more about what that really meant for the Woman at the Well — and what it means for us thirsty women living today.

God Waits for Us in the Unexpected Places

Some years ago my husband, Mike, was interviewing independent Christian musician John Cox, and their conversation turned, believe it or not, toward a napkin and a cassette tape. (I know, my husband — a prolific writer himself — asks the most unusual questions during an interview. You'll have to take up that personality quirk with him!) Anyway, afterward, Mike shared with me the wonderful story that John had told him about those two things, and now I'd like to share it with you.

The story actually began far away from John, in 1992, in a car in a near-empty parking lot. A young woman sat in the car, tired and spent, waiting for who knows what. The needle tracks that dotted her arms revealed the paths she'd taken thus far in her life. This life had left her thirsty, and her futile attempts to quench that thirst had resulted in a deadly dependence on drugs, an addiction that would either kill her or leave her constantly craving more of the substance that wreaked havoc on her mind and body.

But right at this moment, all she wanted to do was sit. And listen. The cassette tape, a gift from a friend, was rolling in the player. On it, a rough-voiced singer and his gritty guitar spoke in a way she couldn't resist.

She turned up the volume. The song was a simple tune called "Don't Look Away." The singer, a guy named John Cox, sang with a passion she could almost touch. He told her — in so many words — she needed God.

"Every time I look around," the lyrics sang, "I start to sink and I'm swallowed by the sea." She caught her breath. *That's me!* she thought, listening harder now, hanging on every word.

Then the chorus finally came around, and the words that spoke were "I hear Jesus say, 'He can't hurt you now. Don't look away, just keep your eyes on me.'"

There was something about that song . . . no, there was something about the Person whom John was singing about. Suddenly she craved that Person, craved what he could bring more than any drug, more than any alcohol, more than anything. And she could sense it: He craved her, too, longed to reach out with his Spirit and quench the thirst that consumed her heart and soul.

Right at that moment, alone in her car, she called out to Jesus, begging him to save her. And right at that moment, joining her in that car, Jesus did. God visited her there, personally and intimately, and the living water of his Holy Spirit filled her soul the way a river fills an arid valley, rushing through with the liquid that brings new life. Never again would drugs control her life. Never again would alcohol dominate her cravings. She'd met God in the most unexpected of places and found that he was all she needed.

Three years later she heard that John Cox was coming to town for a concert, and she knew she had to go. At the concert she could barely control her excitement. This talented singer had such a passion for Jesus, and God had used that passion to bring her to him. But John didn't even know about it . . .

Almost without thinking, she grabbed a napkin and scribbled a story — her story — on it. She couldn't wait; she had to give it to him now.

John says that he still doesn't know her name, but he'll always remember the young woman who interrupted his 1995 concert in Dallas. She was just another face in the crowd until she stood up and began walking toward the stage.

Up front, John was telling a story, making his way through an elaborate introduction of his next song. Suddenly the girl was in front of him, one arm outstretched in John's direction. John wasn't sure how to react at first — after all, it's not every day you find yourself face-to-face with a fan right in the middle of your big intro!

Almost as an afterthought, John noticed the girl was holding something. A napkin. And for some reason she was trying to hand that napkin to John. Right now.

A million thoughts raced through John's mind just then. Was he sweating too much and needed to wipe off? Did he have a smudge on his chin? Was it time to stop so the audience could eat? What?

The surprised musician finally reached for the napkin. Her delivery completed, the girl wordlessly returned to her seat for the rest of the concert. Curiosity piqued, John glanced down at the paper in his hand.

Play the song "Don't Look Away."

He looked again. Yep, it was just a song request. But wait, there was also something more written on the napkin.

Captured by the moment, John nearly forgot where he was and what he was doing as he was mentally transported away, into the story the girl had scribbled on the napkin, delighted that Jesus had used his little cassette tape to orchestrate an unlikely meeting in an unexpected place. Used his song to bring nourishment to a thirsty woman who desperately needed God's love.

When John finished reading the napkin, tears began to stream down his cheeks. Time finally seemed to begin ticking once more as he remembered where he was. Looking over the audience, he finally said, "There's no way I can explain this to you now, so I'm just going to go on to the next song." And then he sang "Don't Look Away."

Reflecting on that moment later, John said in awestruck tones, "That song provided a highway for her to see God directly in front of her. As a musician that's your highest calling right there. That just totally blew me away — and it still does."

Then, with a smile, he adds in closing, "I've still got the napkin."[1]

My friend, that nameless woman in a near-empty parking lot in Somewhere, America, learned anew the lesson the also-anonymous Woman at the Well had experienced long years before:

God waits for us in the unexpected places.

Two millennia ago God unexpectedly waited for the Woman at the Well. He interrupted her daily routine, invaded the depressing existence to which she'd grown comfortable. In 1992 he waited patiently for another thirsty woman in a place she never expected to find him — in the words of a song played through the tinny speakers of her own car stereo.

Today God waits for you and me in the unexpected places too. He breathes in the voices of our loved ones, through the trials that knock the wind out of us, upon the faces of the people we see, in the moments of peace that pop up as welcome respite from the busyness of our schedules and obligations, in the music and laughter and tears that wash over our hopes and dreams, in the pages of his book, the Bible, and more. And here's something else you should know about this unexpected waiting of our Lord . . .

God Goes Out of His Way to Wait for Us

When Jesus showed up at Jacob's well those many years ago, he was on his way from Judea back to Galilee, the place where he had grown to adulthood. Now, during the time that this meeting took place, you should know that Jews and Samaritans despised each other, much the way that Arabs and Jews today live in intense dislike for each other's people group. Listen to how theologian Craig Evans describes this situation:

> By Jesus' day, the regions of Judea and Samaria were separated by bitter tension. Partly based on race and religion, it echoed many centuries of terrible political fights. Therefore when we read that Jesus in passing through the region meets a "Samaritan woman," it means a woman bearing the history, language, religion, and attitudes of people on the far margin of Judaism. A first century reader would barely expect Jesus and the woman to acknowledge each other, much less speak.[2]

In fact this racial and religious animosity showed itself in a geographical way. When a Jew traveled from Judea to Galilee, the shortest way was simply to go in a straight line — heading north across Samaria and into Galilee, which bordered Samaritan territory. But in order to avoid any contact with "unclean" Samaritans (especially Samaritan women who, according to Jewish religious teachers, were "unclean from birth"), typical Jewish travelers would avoid Samaritan territory completely by going east to Jericho, then north before swinging back into Galilee after safely skirting any entry into Samaria. As a matter of fact, Jesus often took this safe route around Samaria and through Jericho during his travels — and that was the route he traveled when he came back to Jerusalem just before his Triumphal Entry and subsequent execution and resurrection.[3]

But this time the normal route was not Jesus' chosen path.

He could have gone the safe route, through Jericho, but instead he went out of his way to cross through hostile territory, to come to a well outside of the city of Sychar, to wait beside that well until an outcast (even among the despised Samaritans!) came to satisfy her thirst. It is almost as if Jesus made a note in his appointment book: *Thursday — Meet Woman at Well. Don't be late.* It would have been easy for the Son of God to avoid that woman on that day, but he didn't do it. Some have suggested that he was just being practical — after all it was shorter to cut through Samaria than to go the scenic route through Jericho.[4] But I think those suggestions do a disservice to the history and personality of the Savior. Why would this trip between Galilee and Judea be any different from his other trips?

I believe there's one reason: A thirsty woman needed the living water that only he could provide. And so he took a road rarely traveled by Jews, entered Samaritan territory, and then parked himself by a well until the Samaritan woman came, unaware, to meet him.

He went out of his way to wait for her. And he does the same for you and me today, finding us in those unexpected places and moments. Now I'm no theologian (although I did go to Bible school if you're into that kind of thing!), but I believe I know why God goes out of his way to wait for us. It's this . . .

God Cherishes Her for Whom He Waits

I know, on the surface it seems that God should not care so deeply for one such as this. After all, this Woman at the Well was no real prize. Were we to judge her by human standards (as the people of her day did), we'd likely say she was damaged goods at best. A woman with a checkered past and piles of emotional scars left over from it — scars that left her spiritually handicapped and helpless. Sin had injured her spirit like war tears apart the body. There was life in there, yes, but what had once been a life filled with potential was now a life stained by symbols of disappointment and limping disability.

And yet, I am here to tell you that God still cherished this broken, thirsty woman.

Let me explain it to you this way, by telling you a story of another broken individual. A story of a British soldier from the eighteenth century, and the lady who waited for his return to her arms . . .

The lady caught her breath when she saw the letter. A smile sneaked onto her lips when she saw the name attached to it. It was from her love, her fiancé now so far from his home in England. He had gone to the Americas to fight for the Crown in what the colonists were calling a war for independence.

Before he left, he'd made his love known, and the soldier and the lady had joyously agreed to marry. They would wed after the war, and live happily ever after, she was sure.

The lady hurried her way to a private place and gently tore open the page from her love. At first the smile froze on her face, then, wearily, it crept away completely and was soon replaced by tears.

The words on the page revealed a man in great pain, both

physical and emotional. He had been wounded, he said, during battle. Badly wounded. In fact he had lost a leg completely, and in his eyes he had become less than a man.

"I am disfigured and maimed," he wrote, "and so changed from when you last saw me." And then with heartbreaking courage, he wrote that he now released her from her pledge to marry, breaking off their engagement and urging her to find another man.

A whole man . . .

The soldier caught his breath when he saw the letter. In truth he had longed for it to come but felt certain it never would. And he feared its coming as well, because it could only mean tears. But he clutched it anyway. It was from the lady he loved and had once pledged to marry, the Englishwoman who had vowed to wait out a war for him.

She is so beautiful, he thought, remembering her hair, her smile, the gentle touch of her hand. *And she is no longer mine.*

Silently he ripped open the note, disappointment etched upon his face. At first the sorrow froze there, then, quietly, it crept away completely and was soon replaced with a smile.

She is so beautiful, he thought, remembering nothing of her appearance and instead gazing deeply into her heart. For in the letter she spoke again of her love, hotly denying the suggestion that she would end her engagement to the now-crippled soldier. He read the letter once more, stopping on the line that held his heart.

"I will marry you," his lady wrote firmly, "as long as there is enough body left to hold your soul."[5]

Do you see what I am trying to show you, dear friend? What the Woman at the Well first revealed for us so many, many years ago?

God waits for you in the unexpected places of your life.

God goes out of his way to wait for you to meet him, to enjoy him, to discover the life that he has for you.

God cherishes you, the one for whom he waits.

Drink deeply, my sister, of these truths. They are life to your heart and health to your bones. They are sweet droplets of water for the thirsty woman's soul.

And they are just the beginning . . .

experiencing the unexpected

When a Samaritan woman came to draw water, Jesus said to
her, "Will you give me a drink?" . . . The Samaritan woman
said to him, "You are a Jew and I am a Samaritan woman. How
can you ask me for a drink?" (For Jews do not associate
with Samaritans.)

—JOHN 4:7-9

"A stranger," she whispered to herself.

This was a surprise — and not a pleasant one. He's a Jew, no
less, *she thought.* Sitting by the well. By *my* well. Right now, of all
times, when normally this place would be safely empty.

*She sighed and contemplated her next move. Should she try to
wait him out? To linger here in the distance until he'd had enough
and moved on? He looked like a traveler; surely he wouldn't stay
here long. But it was not likely that he was traveling alone either.
So where were his companions? And how many were there?*

*She turned her head and scanned the outline of the city nearby,
but the midday silhouettes gave no clue as to what visitors might*

be concealed within them. She turned back to the man and saw his face was now upturned, eyes closed, a faint smile on his lips. Was he praying? Or just relaxing in the momentary silence of his resting spot?

The stranger's head dipped just a bit, and his eyes flashed open, instantly meeting her gaze—almost as if he had seen her before—blinking awake in her direction.

The faint smile remained.

She looked away and felt her pulse quicken just a bit. A sticky, uncomfortable perspiration formed in her palms. Everyone knew the Jews hated Samaritans, and to be honest, she felt no kindness toward Jews in return. Yet here this intruder sat, blocking her access to the one thing she needed most: water.

Yes, she was thirsty.

She ran her tongue over dry lips, still unsure of her next move. If she left now, she could go home and take a chance that she could come safely to the well later in the day. But as the day ran longer, the risks grew greater; women from the town would begin making an evening trip to the well, getting a fresh supply of liquid for evening meals and nighttime duties. A few men might also stop by the well on their way in from the fields, pausing long enough for one good drink to end the day. And who knew when this stranger's companions would finally return, or whether they would decide to camp by the well for the night?

Finally it was the scratching at the back of her throat that made the decision. She was so thirsty. And at this time of day, this was her well; this was her place. Stranger or no, that water belonged to her and she intended to get it.

Besides, *she reasoned softly to herself,* he is a Jew. It would be against his laws to even speak to me, a Samaritan woman.

She dared to glance back toward Jacob's well and saw that the stranger hadn't moved — and that his eyes were still fixed on her. Well, that was nothing new, she decided. Men often looked hungrily at her, though they usually tried to cover their interest more carefully than this man did. She straightened her back, adjusted her jar, and stepped confidently toward the well once more.

In a few paces she stood near the stranger and felt relieved when his gaze finally turned away from her and toward the desert horizon. She busied herself in preparation for filling her water jar, and already her mind was beginning to wander back to the list of chores waiting to fill her afternoon and evening.

"Would you give me a drink of water?"

She fairly jumped at the sound of his voice. It seemed to come from all around her, disorienting her at first, until she finally understood that the words had come from the mouth of the man next to her. She looked slowly in his direction and was surprised to find that he was still staring into the horizon. An awkward silence hung between them, yet he seemed completely at ease, waiting for her to respond.

At first she felt a little flustered at the unexpected casualness of the request. He spoke as if he knew her, as if they were already friends. Then a glittering annoyance began to decorate her thinking. Who did this man think he was? How dare he interrupt her daily chore for his own presumptive ends? And who did he think she was? His servant? His slave? She had another Man who laid that kind of claim to her, and that Man was at least willing to work in the fields for her in return. And besides, this stranger must also be a hypocrite, for Jewish law forbade him from associating with her. Yet now, when no one was looking, he was all too willing to break those rules, to talk to her and even to drink water touched by her supposedly unclean hands.

She drew herself up, leaned into his line of vision and, for the first time, looked directly into his eyes.

"How come you, a Jew, are asking me, a Samaritan woman, for a drink?"

She did not say the rest of what she was thinking, but it was apparent nonetheless. Everyone knows that a real Jew wouldn't be caught dead talking to a Samaritan. And everyone knows that Jews and Samaritans are enemies. Why would you expect me, your enemy, to fill your throat with water? To do anything generous for you at all?

The stranger simply smiled, like a magician hiding something up his sleeve.

How do you prepare for the unexpected? For the moment when God himself is going to throw a surprise into your mundane existence?

I find this quality of Christ — his element of surprise — both alluring and frustrating in my own life, and I can only imagine what must have been going through the mind of the Woman at the Well when Jesus orchestrated a surprising interruption in the timeline of her existence. Sure, I know how this story ends — and I feel excited for this woman because I know what is to come for her. But at that moment, on that specific dry, dusty day beside Jacob's well at Sychar, this poor woman knew nothing of the surprise being laid out for her.

Today when we read the histories of Scripture, we are often

guilty of what my friend Larry Shallenberger calls "playing to the end." Listen to how he describes this:

During my single years, I dabbled in acting at a local community theater. One of the cardinal sins of acting, I learned, is to "play to the end." An actor can ruin a play if, in Scene One, he wears emotions on his face that don't belong until late in Act Two. For example, early in the play the *actor* may know his character will kill his wife moments before Intermission; but in that moment the *character* only knows he is feeling extra possessive of his wife. If the actor prematurely pastes a guilty look on his face, he'll tip off the audience and rob them of their sense of mystery.

I have to confess, having grown up in the church and having read the Bible dozens of times, I've robbed myself of the mystery and suspense that saturates the book. I can read the book "playing to the end." For instance, in Acts chapter 12, there's no need to fear for Peter or the future of the church as Peter festers in a strange prison; I know that an angel is going to orchestrate a jailbreak just verses later. My pulse rate remains constant as I take in the shipwrecks, the tongues of fire, and the riots; they all have a ho-hum familiarity. I don't patrol the pages of the Bible with Marine-like vigilance, scanning my environment for the next explosion. Instead, I saunter through it as if it were just another walk down the streets of Erie, PA.

It wasn't like that for the early church. They couldn't play to the end. Every day held new mystery and terror.

Peter didn't know that Ananias would die at the sound of his voice (Acts 5:1-11). All Peter intended to do was confront Ananias for lying. At the end of the day, Peter had to live with the fact that God had used him to execute two people.

Later, when Peter sat chained in a humid stone prison cell, he expected to die in the morning (Acts 12:1-19). An angelic intervention was more than he could have ever hoped for . . .

The events of the Bible, methodically planned by God, were shocking to the people who found themselves enfolded within them. We need to learn to breathe in the emotions that took place in the moment — wonder, delight, fear, confidence, and sometimes even offense and horror.

God's random acts are not safe.[1]

I must confess that when I read about that first, surprising exchange between Jesus and the Woman at the Well described in John 4:7-9, I am guilty of "playing to the end." But today, right now, instead of reading comfortably, secure in the happy ending, I long to place myself squarely into this woman's historical, personal experience. And when I do, I find that I discover not the end of her story, but the surprising, inconvenient, religiously subversive beginning to a relationship between a thirsty person and an unsafe Savior.

It's in this moment that I begin to glimpse the unpredictable truths about the personality of God — and I am struck by the image of Christ as the perpetrator of the unexpected within the confines of routine life.

God Is a Surprising Personality

This statement, "God is a surprising personality," is something of a surprise for me to think — and to write — about God. It invokes in my mind the image of Jesus almost as a prankster, or as a mischievous child, and that seems to do a disservice to the grandeur and glory of the King of kings and Lord of lords.

Still, my human limitations in understanding (and imagination!) cannot change the truth of those words. God *is* a surprising person. He does act in ways that defy predictability, that even could be called subversive.

It's impossible to overstate the enormity of the offense when Jesus initiated this conversation with the Woman at the Well. It's impossible to understate the shocked reaction this woman must have had upon hearing this strange, hated Jew ask her for a drink of water. Remember in chapter 1 of this book how we discovered the inherent hostility and religious condemnation with which all God-fearing, pious Jews treated Samaritan women? It would have been out of place for them to even nod at each other or make eye contact.

In that day and time, on that road, at that well by the city of Sychar, by all moral standards in the religious and national community of Israel, *the right thing* for Jesus to do would have been to simply ignore this trashy Samaritan woman who came sashaying to the well. Even worse, *the absolute wrong thing* for Jesus to do would have been to speak to her, to engage her in a familiar, friendly conversation. Any ten-year-old child would have known that.

The Woman at the Well knew that.

Jesus knew that.

And he not only ignored the moral and national edicts of his people and of that time — he cast them aside with the force of an iron-fisted challenge from God himself toward the intolerant, stupid customs that ruled the religion and lifestyles of those who were supposed to be God's most ardent followers.

Surprise!

How do you react to something like that? To the flagrant rebellion against the supposed God by the one true God? Especially if, like this unsuspecting woman, you are caught in the crosshairs between what is expected and what is true, but you are unsure which one is which?

I can't say I've had that kind of deep, core-shattering kind of surprise in my life yet, but having married the man I did, I can say that I've had my share of the unpredictable. In fact I got another taste of it just this week.

At the time I am writing this, my husband, Mike, is forty-three years old. He's well established in his career, the father of a teenager, and pretty much settled in his ways. In fact, after twenty years of marriage, I can usually tell what he's thinking, what he's feeling, who he likes and dislikes, what kinds of clothes he will wear, or even which DVD he's going to pick up from the five-dollar bin at Wal-Mart. Not long ago I was finishing one of his sentences for him, and he paused, looked at me, and said, "I'm not as tame as you think I am." We both laughed, and I forgot all about it.

Until Sunday.

Over Father's Day weekend Mike took our son to Dallas to hang out with friends and just do "guy stuff" like playing cards, going to movies, sightseeing, attending an arena football game, and the like. It's a guy reunion that Mike and Tony and their friends have been doing annually for the past six or seven years. Usually they come back with a few souvenirs and some fun stories about their experiences on the road.

This year Mike came back with a tattoo of the Superman logo on his arm.

Did I mention that this is a middle-aged, slightly balding man with body hair blanketing his skin from shoulder to foot? Did I mention that he's spent the last five years telling Tony, our teenage son, in no uncertain terms that there was no way Tony would be allowed to do something "permanently scarring to his skin" like getting a tattoo? In fact his favorite line on the subject has always been, "You wouldn't put a bumper sticker on a Rolls-Royce would you?"

Surprise!

It turns out my husband is not the predictable guy that I had come to believe he was![2] And likewise, God is not the predictable religious monarch we so often expect him to be either.

Remember the woman's reaction when Jesus confronted her at the well? "How come you, a Jew, are asking me, a Samaritan woman, for a drink?" she said.

She knew what was expected. She knew the routine, the way that the world worked in her day. And in her question we see that she, too, was unprepared for the surprising and — I'm going to say it — the mischievously holy nature of God as it is so often displayed in human life. But honestly, at this point, shouldn't we come to expect the unexpected with God? Consider:

- Before the beginning of time, God yawned into the emptiness of nonexistence and simply decided that something should be there. Six days later, all of creation teemed with life! (Genesis 1:1–2:3)
- When God first confronted Moses, he spoke through the fiery brambles of burning (but not burned) shrubbery. Would you have expected that? (Exodus 3)
- When God wanted to give courage to Ezekiel, he led the prophet to a stinking, filthy, parched valley filled with forgotten bones of long-dead men. Then — without the aid of Hollywood green screens or any special effects (and in what I think must have also been a disgusting and macabre experience) — God miraculously filled those dead, decaying bones with human organs and then layered muscle and tendon and skin and hair upon them to create a living, breathing army of souls. (Ezekiel 37)
- When God wanted to redeem the world and save us from our sins, he implanted his very being into the reproductive system of a peasant girl, a virgin who unexpectedly conceived the Savior of the world. (Luke 2)

I think the Woman at the Well learned — and I am just beginning to discover — that God is not safe. Christ is not tame. He who shaped the laws of nature is free to bend the natural so that it conforms at his whim to his supernatural purpose. The One who imposed the laws of nature and the normal way of life is also a master of surprise.

So why would Christ, a Jew, ask the woman, a Samaritan, for water? I can almost imagine that Jesus' eyes twinkled when she asked him that question, that a grin might have formed on his lips when he heard it spoken. And in my sanctified imagination I can practically hear him thinking, "Because, dearest daughter, I have a surprise that I've painstakingly prepared just for you."

God's Surprises Are Always Good, but Not Always Comfortable

Yes, God is certainly a surprising personality, if only because he knows so much and we understand so little. And when he, infinity incarnate, chooses to rivet his attention and his purpose upon the finite moments of your life and mine, the result can often be jarring.

I'm sure the Woman at the Well felt something of the incomprehensible as her emotions and experience struggled to grasp the surprising actions of Christ when he spoke directly to her — in violation of the basic custom and legalities of that day and place. While I can't know with certainty what went through her mind, I can tell you that I, too, have experienced some of the incomprehensibility of Christ's actions in my life.

I hope you'll pardon me now, as I am about to tell you a very personal story.

Several years ago I was diagnosed with what doctors call "secondary infertility." Basically what this means is that although I was able to conceive and deliver a first child (my wonderful son, Tony!), after his birth I became infertile, unlikely to conceive or unable to bring a child to full term. Now, as the oldest of five kids, I come from a large family, and I fully expected to have my own adult home filled with four or five kids of my own.

Surprise! This was not God's plan for me. In fact, after two heartbreaking miscarriages, my body simply refused to conceive a new child. It was a difficult time in my life, but my husband and I finally determined to be grateful for the one child that God had given us, rather than to be bitter about the ones he had not.

Then the unexpected happened. A young, single woman I'd met in Arizona approached me with the news that she was pregnant. "Amy," she said with pleading in her voice, "would you adopt my baby?"

I was stunned. Then overjoyed. I talked it over with Mike and we both were thrilled to step in and adopt this child that God was forming inside the womb of that young woman. Just when we had given up, God, it seemed, had brought a beautiful surprise into our lives.

Our son was in elementary school at the time, and when we told him the news, he could hardly contain his excitement over the idea of finally having a little brother on the way. In fact he cleared out half of his own bedroom to make space for a crib and changing table where he would share a room with his new baby brother.

We connected with an adoption agency to handle all the details of the process and discovered that, financially, we faced a serious obstacle. We simply didn't have the money needed to pay for this adoption, and my husband was too obstinate to ask for donations from anyone.

"We will pray about it," he said. "And if someone asks, we'll tell them of the need. But otherwise we'll keep it between us and God, and see what God will do."

I wasn't happy with that approach at all.

Until, out of nowhere, money started showing up in our mailbox.

"We were praying and felt God leading us to send you this check," said some notes. "We heard you were adopting a baby and wanted to contribute to your expenses," said others. People handed us cash at church; friends stopped by the house with envelopes of money. We never asked anyone but God for anything — yet God miraculously brought this money into our hands. On the very day when our payment was due, a final check arrived that was exactly the amount we needed to reach our financial goal. We were overjoyed once more. God had not only provided, he'd done so in dynamic fashion!

As the baby's due date grew closer, we could barely contain ourselves. We picked out a name for our new child. We set up his bedroom. We made travel arrangements for when it was time to fly to Arizona to pick up our child. And then the call came . . .

"Amy," the young woman's voice said through the phone line, "I've decided to keep this baby. I've decided not to put him up for adoption after all."

Surprise. Agonizing, gut-wrenching surprise.

When we got the call, Tony had just gone to bed. We knew he could hear us talking and decided that he deserved to know the truth as well. So Mike went into his room, sat on the side of his bed, and told him the news. Then he spent the next two hours holding our fragile, only son, while he cried himself to sleep.

I still feel heartbreak whenever I remember this time in my life. And yet, in spite of my loss, I would never fault a woman for choosing to keep her own child. About a year after his birth, we had a gathering with friends, and this young woman and her toddler were there. He was healthy, happy, and I was glad to see this. At one point he walked over to Mike and raised up his hands, asking to be held. So Mike obliged, holding the child in his lap and whispering in his ear to make him laugh.

"Wow, he never does that," the mother said quietly to me when she saw her toddler with Mike. "He never gets near to strangers."

I looked at Mike holding the contented boy. *That's no stranger*, I thought to myself. *That's the man who could have been his father.*

I've never seen that child or his mother since, but I've often cried out in anger and frustration to God over the whole experience.

I wasn't seeking to adopt, God! I've shouted. *I didn't ask for this; you brought it into my life. When the money would have prevented us from adopting, you miraculously provided all the funds we needed. What in the world were you doing at that time, with me in that place? How come you, the Father, were asking me, a barren woman, to be this child's mother? And why, at the last moment, did you take this child away from me?*

I don't exactly know the answers to those questions. But I have learned something very important:

God's surprises are good, but they are not always comfortable.

My Father is not tame. He intercedes in my life in the way he thinks best, whether I like it or not. He breaks the rules of my perceived fairness; he whisks me along with him into adventures I'd rather not experience. Just as Christ unsettled the Woman at the Well by asking her for water, he often makes me unsure and anxious with the things he asks of me and the way his plans play out in my life.

He rarely makes me comfortable. But his surprises are always good.

Several years after this failed adoption experience, my husband and I were talking. "You know," he said to me. "It's obvious to me that God orchestrated those events in our lives. I can't say I really know why he did this. But I wonder sometimes what might have happened if we hadn't been willing to step up and promise to adopt that child. Or if we had dropped out of the adoption process because we didn't have enough money.

"At both those points in time, it's very possible that this young woman might have chosen to abort that beautiful child. Perhaps we were not meant to parent that boy; maybe we were just brought in to make sure he had a chance at life."

Surprise.

Yes, I think it may be true. It's possible that my short heartbreak was necessary simply to ensure that this child was born. If that was God's surprise, then right now, today, let me tell you that it was worth every tear and every moment of grief I endured, and I feel privileged to have been a tool God used in this way.

You Are God's Biggest Surprise

I've monopolized your attention for too long in this chapter, I know. So let me finish this conversation by sharing with you one last thing I see in this captured moment between Jesus and the Woman at the Well.

Yes, God is a surprising person. Yes, his surprises are

sometimes uncomfortable. But I think you should know that *you* are his biggest surprise. Let me explain.

When Jesus asked this woman for a drink of water, her surprised response was, "How come you, a Jew, are asking me, a Samaritan woman, for a drink?"

This was a legitimate question, and the obvious answers simply don't add up.

Did Jesus ask her this because he was really thirsty? Apparently not. If you read the rest of this story, you will see that he never got a drink from the woman, and in fact he seemed to quickly forget that initial request.

Did he ask her for a drink because he was incapable of getting a drink for himself? Obviously not. He was physically healthy enough to walk from Judea to Galilee, so obviously he could hoist a bucket of water out of a well.

Did he ask because he was so arrogant that he wanted a servant to fetch him a drink? Well, the answer to that question appears to be no as well. After all, his own disciples had been at the well with him earlier, and in only moments they would be returning to be with him at the well again. If his ego had needed a servant, any one of them would have surely sufficed.

So why did Jesus, a Jew, ask her, a Samaritan woman, for a drink? Andrew Snaden, in his beautiful book, *When God Met a Girl*, has an interesting theory.

> Since the cultural norm at that time was that men didn't
> talk to women in public . . . he had to have a reason
> to speak to her. The reason Jesus created was thirst.
> Thirst was probably the only icebreaker Jesus could use
> to initiate a conversation with her that wouldn't have

caused [the Woman at the Well] to take off running.

This could certainly be a part of the truth of this situation, but I suspect that Jesus had more in his thinking than only an icebreaker strategy.

I think the request was actually for *her*, not for him. I think it was because the surprise he had up his sleeve was not that she could help him, but that he could transform her, from the inside out, with rivers of living water.

In short I think *she* was God's big surprise at that moment — who she had been, who she was, and who she would be with Christ in her life. We'll talk more deeply about this in the rest of this book, but for now let me tell you one last story that might help to explain what I mean. It's a story that is dear to me, because it is about my own uncle, Ken Wakefield.

Like the Woman at the Well, the first time he met Jesus, Ken was a wreck — emotionally, physically, spiritually. He was trapped by the debilitating effects of years of alcohol abuse and a lifetime of unhealthy living.

It was a Sunday morning when Ken found himself thrown (in the spiritual sense) into an unexpected encounter with Jesus Christ himself. Ken stood, unwashed and unkempt, in front of the shaving mirror in his home and felt that today would be a good day to visit a church, though he hadn't been to one for some time.

He had traveled a long road on his way to this particular shaving mirror. While he was a child, he witnessed his mother suffering as a victim of verbal spousal abuse for years. Finally Ken's mom could stand it no longer.

"I can't take any more of this," she told him when he was

fourteen. That summer of 1947, she took Ken's younger brother and sister and fled from the rest of her family and the farm that was her home.

Ken was left behind — but unwanted and unhappy at his home. A month or so later, young Ken and his older brother also ran away from the farm, reuniting with their mother at a relative's place.

It was during that brief stay at an aunt and uncle's house that Ken first heard bits and pieces of the good news about Jesus Christ. Ken's uncle and aunt attended a church in the tiny community of Buena Vista, New York. Ken remembers the preacher talking about a person being saved, but the word was confusing. What in the world did it mean to be saved? Too shy to ask for more information, he left the church with his questions unanswered. Ken then moved to the country to live with his grandfather and grandmother. Being a strong teenager, he loved to work in the fields with his granddad.

The transition to adulthood was not easy, however. Soon he discovered alcohol, and it seemed to be an instant cure for all his insecurities. A couple of drinks chased away his shyness, making him feel he was ready to tackle anything.

What Ken didn't realize was that one day he'd have to tackle an addiction to the alcohol that soon took over his life. By the time he recognized the danger, Ken was trapped — a slave to the addicting power of drink. It dictated what he thought about, where he went, whom he associated with, and how he behaved. He finally had to speak the horrifying words, "I am an alcoholic."

Ken knew he was in trouble. "All I could picture," he recalls, "was that I was on a very high slide, going down real fast, and soon I would hit bottom and be in hell."

By now Ken was grown and married, with a house full of his own children. One particular Saturday everything seemed to fall apart. Ken's wife was ill in the hospital. Coming home from visiting with her, Ken was deeply depressed, so much so that he seriously contemplated suicide. For him it seemed the only realistic solution. Sitting on the couch with his head in his hands, he felt he'd hit the bottom. It couldn't get any worse than this.

It was there that God chose to meet Ken Wakefield.

Suddenly, unexpectedly, Ken had a distinct sense of the Lord speaking to his heart. The words he heard deep within his soul were, "Ken, if you do what I ask, I'll get you out of this mess."

Ken was both scared and excited. His immediate reaction was to call on his Christian neighbors, Vi and Ab, and tell them what had happened. When Ken showed up at their front door, this godly couple stopped what they were doing and took the time needed to explain to their alcoholic neighbor who Jesus is, the story of Jesus' power over sin, and the availability of Christ's forgiving love for his life. Then they prayed with Ken and he went home.

Nothing happened, it seemed. No skyrockets, no lightning flashing or earth trembling. Though no longer suicidal, Ken felt almost the same as before. He was actually a little disappointed. Shrugging his shoulders, he went to bed.

The next morning, Sunday morning, Ken got up to get ready for church and . . . well, maybe I'd better let Ken tell what happened next:

When I got up, I decided to visit Vi and Ab's church. I went into the bathroom to shave. When I looked in the mirror, I realized that this was the first morning I could remember when I didn't *have* to have a drink.

I started to feel a warmth that began at my feet and rose slowly to the top of my head. I felt as though I was being unzipped from head to toe and someone was hosing me out with a big hose! I felt clean! (And I still have the feeling.)

That oppressive weight of guilt Ken had carried for so long seemed to fall off his back. A profound sense of freedom swept over him. It was then that he knew Jesus had saved his soul, had revitalized his heart, had refused to let him continue down that slide to destruction. And he realized that God had forgiven him — *forever.*

Ken Wakefield chuckles today at the thought of that Sunday morning in front of the shaving mirror. "From that day on," he reports, "a glass of beer had the same appeal to me as a glass of motor oil!"[4]

Surprise.

When Jesus Christ met my Uncle Ken, he did more than simply save his soul, more than just forgive his sins. He did for him what is promised in 2 Corinthians 5:17: "If anyone is in Christ, he is a new creation; the old has gone, the new has come!"

So, dear sister, keep this little bit of truth in your heart: You are the reason Jesus keeps injecting just a bit of the unexpected into this otherwise mundane world. For in the end, the wonderful change — the "new creation" — that he intends to showcase in your life is truly his greatest surprise.

teasing the mystery

Jesus answered her, "If you knew the gift of God and who it is that asks you for a drink, you would have asked him and he would have given you living water."

"Sir," the woman said, "you have nothing to draw with and the well is deep. Where can you get this living water? Are you greater than our father Jacob, who gave us the well and drank from it himself, as did also his sons and his flocks and herds?"

Jesus answered, "Everyone who drinks this water will be thirsty again, but whoever drinks the water I give him will never thirst. Indeed, the water I give him will become in him a spring of water welling up to eternal life."

—JOHN 4:10-14

She felt herself torn. On the one hand it felt good to look this Jew straight in the eye and challenge the smug superiority of those religious hypocrites in Israel. On the other hand this stranger didn't seem to deserve the harsh accusation she'd just implied. To look at him, she would guess he was a rabbi of some sort. Perhaps it was a good thing that a Jewish rabbi would break with his religious tradition and speak on friendly terms with a Samaritan woman.

Then again, perhaps he had something in mind besides simple race relations.

Her eyes narrowed while she waited for the man to move out of the way. Was he going to just sit there and assume that she would serve him like his own private little slave girl? Who did this arrogant invader think he was? And who did he think she was?

A familiar anger washed through her, the kind that she'd spilled out in the past on her lovers, her enemies, and even on God, if he were listening at all. She finally settled into a satisfied smirk, glaring at the stranger with eyes that spoke her thoughts. You are a fraud, she whispered toward him from inside her head. A religious leader who doesn't even follow the traditions of all the Jewish rabbis before you. Now get out of my way and let me finish this chore in peace.

She was so thirsty.

The stranger leaned back comfortably. He almost seemed to shrug, but he made no move toward the well, nor toward any of the tools that would allow him to allay his desire for water. In fact, for someone who had just asked for a drink, he seemed remarkably unconcerned about actually receiving the contents of the well.

When he spoke, it was with surprising familiarity, as if he had known her since she was a little girl. She searched her memory. Had she met this man before? Had they once been friends?

"If you knew the gift of God," he said calmly, "and who it is that asks you for a drink, you would have asked him and he *would have given you living water."*

What was that supposed to mean?

She didn't even take a moment to consider the rabbi's gibber-ish; she didn't have to. It was absurd talk, and she had no time for childish games like this.

"Sir," she said with dripping disdain, "you have nothing to draw with and the well is deep. Where can you get this 'living' water?"

She should stop there, she reasoned to herself. But something about this stranger just got under her skin, something about the way he carried himself, the way he acted as if he owned the whole world and her inside it. It was too much, and she couldn't resist one last jab in his direction.

"Are you greater than our father Jacob, who gave us the well and drank from it himself, as did also his sons and his flocks and herds?"

There. That should put this Jew in his place. Maybe now he'd leave her alone. Or maybe not.

The look in his eyes was neither fear nor anger. Was it pity? No. It was . . . patience. Like he was about to explain something very simple to a child who just wouldn't listen. At any rate he didn't hesitate.

"Everyone who drinks this water will be thirsty again," he said, "but whoever drinks the water I give him will never thirst. Indeed, the water I give him will become in him a spring of water welling up to eternal life."

A breath caught in the back of her throat. That made abso-lutely no sense. Or did it?

Could there be such a thing as this living water? And did this man indeed have access to it? She let her eyes relax, opening just enough to reveal a curiosity that was now beginning to grow within her. This mystery man was certainly different from most others she'd met.

And she was so thirsty.

Were I to have been present at the time and place where Jesus intervened in the life of the Woman at the Well, I think I might have been more than a bit confused by the enigmatic conversation I was having with this person sitting before me. What at first seemed a commonplace moment (a trip to get water) was fast becoming a rush of secrets and — let's be honest — near absurdity.

The stranger who asked for a drink from the well was now claiming to possess some kind of mythical "living" water? Get serious. Either he was crazy . . . or there was some great mystery that he understood and I did not.

Ah, the mystery. Life, especially when God is involved, is so often a mystery, isn't it? I think one of my favorite commentaries on mystery comes from the 1998 movie *Shakespeare in Love*. In this Oscar-winning film, a young Will Shakespeare (played by Joseph Fiennes) struggles to complete his now-famous play, *Romeo and Juliet*. Alongside him, his benefactor and producer, Philip Henslowe (Geoffrey Rush), struggles to keep merciless creditors at bay long enough to debut young Will's new stage production. One particularly brutal creditor is Hugh Fennyman (Tom Wilkinson), a blackguard whose money-collection techniques include placing his debtors' feet into a burning fire, cutting off noses and ears, and quite possibly murdering clients for nonpayment.

At a pivotal point in this film, a royal decree has been issued to shut down all theaters in London until further notice, meaning that Henslowe can't put on Shakespeare's play, which in turn means that he can't sell tickets to Shakespeare's new play, which means that it is now impossible for Henslowe to pay his debt to the sadistic Fennyman. And so it happens that, while walking peacefully through the marketplace, Henslowe suddenly finds himself in the clutches of Hugh Fennyman and his murderous henchmen.

"What have I done, Mr. Fennyman?" Henslowe stutters while being forcefully dragged across the square.

"The theaters have all been closed down by the plague," snaps Fennyman.

"Oh, that," says Henslowe.

"By order of the Master of the Revels," Fennyman says, emphasizing the severity of the shutdown and noting its royal source.

"Mr. Fennyman," says Henslowe, pausing just long enough to endure being slammed up against a hard wooden beam, "allow me to explain about the theater business. The natural condition is one of insurmountable obstacles on the road to imminent disaster."

"So what do we do?" asks Fennyman.

"Nothing," says Henslowe. "Strangely enough, it all turns out well."

"How?" seethes Fennyman.

"I don't know," says Henslowe. "*It's a mystery.*"

At that moment a bell rings in the square and a royal herald walks past shouting the newest development: "The theaters are reopened by order of the Master of the Revels! The theaters are reopened."

While his captors stand with open mouths, staring in wonder at the new turn of events, Henslowe gently extricates himself from their clutches and happily walks away with a promise that Shakespeare's play is soon to be ready.[1]

It's a mystery . . .

Those words ring true for so much of my life! Granted, I don't often have to face down bloodthirsty debt collectors the way that poor Mr. Henslowe did, but I do often find myself face-to-face with the normal worries and threats of modern living. When I find myself in some new calamity of health or career or parenthood or daughterhood or finances or spiritual disruption, I often throw up my hands and seethe, *So what do we do now, God?* And at the oddest times, during prayer or worry or both, for some reason this silly scene from a Hollywood love story pops into my head, and I can almost hear God laughing behind the tones of Geoffrey Rush's voice:

Nothing, the Soul Whisperer says to my disconcerted heart. *Strangely enough, it all turns out well.*

I expect that, when Christ started babbling about living water, the Woman at the Well felt a little like poor old Henslowe and I do — confused and at a loss for what to do or expect next.

An interesting sidelight to the mystery of this moment for the Woman at the Well lies in Jesus' initial, unexpected request for water, and then in the mysterious suggestion of the living water that he offered to her in return. Bible historians tell us that, in the Middle Eastern culture of Jesus' day, "one of the first things done for a guest was to give him a drink of cool water. It was a pledge of friendship."[2] In that cultural context one has to wonder if, by asking for a drink of water, Jesus was also tacitly asking for a pledge of friendship from this woman. And by revealing that he had living water to give, was he also offering to this woman a pledge of eternal friendship? Did this Woman at the Well understand that an eternal friendship was being offered and requested? It's possible, but given the out-of-the-blue element of this particular situation in her life, I'm guessing it's not likely that she picked up all these theological nuances. At least not at that moment.

You see, while staring into the face of Christ, this woman was actually looking into the eyes of the universe's greatest mystery, of the One whose mere existence was beyond anything she could ever hope to understand or imagine. And strangely enough, it all turned out well for this woman, almost as if God himself had planned it that way.

We Need Mystery in Life

I think it is no accident that Jesus used the element of mystery to draw in the Woman at the Well. After all, he is God, and he knew two thousand years ago what educators and behavioral experts could not verify until recently: Human nature loves a mystery.

Think of it this way. Let's say you and I are standing in front of a table. On the table are three boxes. Two of the boxes have clear plastic lids that allow you to see what's inside. There's a diamond necklace in one box and an extravagant emerald ring in the other. The third box is wrapped like a Christmas present and is about the same size as the other two boxes.

"Each box on this table, including the gift-wrapped one, is valued at one thousand dollars," I say to you. "Now, as my gift, you can choose any one of these boxes to have as your own. The contents of that wrapped box will remain unseen unless you choose that as your gift. You have ten minutes to make your decision."

Over the course of the next ten minutes, which of these three boxes will you spend the most time inspecting?

If you are like the rest of us, you'll look admiringly at the diamond necklace and emerald ring, but you will spend the bulk of your time carefully examining the gift-wrapped box, shaking it, feeling its weight in your hands, pressing its sides, checking for any tears in the wrapping paper, maybe even sneaking a quick sniff to see if you can solve the mystery of what's inside that last box. And, at the end of ten minutes (unless you have an overriding attraction to diamonds or emeralds), you will most likely choose the gift-wrapped box. Why? Because even though you like diamonds and emeralds, you, simply by virtue of the fact that you are human, have an ingrained attraction to the mystery represented by that gift-wrapped box. In short your curiosity will overrule your knowledge, driving you to feel like you *must* know what is hidden inside that last box.

This kind of experience is what some scientists and marketing gurus call the "gap theory of curiosity." According to behavioral economist George Loewenstein of Carnegie Mellon University, curiosity is the result of noticing a gap in our knowledge — a gap that subsequently causes us intellectual pain, like having an itch that needs to be scratched. In order to alleviate that intellectual itch, we strive to fill the gap with more knowledge, thus satisfying our curiosity and solving our intellectual mysteries.[3]

Marketing strategists Chip and Dan Heath explored Loewenstein's theory and applied it to the way we consume modern media. Listen to their insightful commentary:

> We sit patiently through bad movies, even though they may be painful to watch, because it's too painful not to know how they end . . .
>
> Most local news programs run teaser ads for upcoming broadcasts. The teasers preview the lead story in laughably hyperbolic terms: "There's a new drug sweeping the teenage community — and it may be in your own medicine cabinet!" "Which famous local restaurant was just cited — for slime in the ice machine?" . . .
>
> These are sensationalist examples of the gap theory. They work because they tease you with something that you don't know — in fact, something that you didn't care about at all, until you found out that you didn't know it.[4]

I would be reluctant to call Jesus a sensationalist (though some of his miracles might argue otherwise), but when I look at the conversation he initiated with the Woman at the Well, I can't help but feel that he was very much aware of what Loewenstein and the two Heaths would centuries later call the "gap theory of curiosity."

"If you knew," Jesus said to the woman, "the gift of God and who it is that asks you for a drink, you would have asked him and he would have given you living water."

Do you see all the ways that Jesus is teasing out the mystery for this woman? The way he is drawing her to him with a hint of something she doesn't know — something, in fact, she didn't care about at all until she found out that she didn't know it? His one simple statement of fact so clearly reverberates with intellectual "itches," creating questions that demand to be answered by the sudden gaps of knowledge inside her mind.

Do you know the gift of God?

Do you know just whom this is that you are talking to?

What exactly is living water? Can there actually be such a thing?

And if there is such a thing as living water, can this stranger really possess it — and give it away?

And even if he did have this water, how would he give it to me?

Just who is this strange man, anyway?

It's a mystery — and one that wasn't lost on this curious, thirsty woman.

"Sir," she said in response, "you have nothing to draw with and the well is deep. Where can you get this living water? Are you greater than our father Jacob, who gave us the well and drank from it himself, as did also his sons and his flocks and herds?"

Knowing what you now know about human nature, does it surprise you at all that this woman's immediate reaction to the mystery of Christ's words was to ask questions that would fill her knowledge gap? "Where can you get this? Are you greater than our father Jacob?"

And knowing what you know about Christ, would you be surprised to find out that those were the kinds of questions he wanted her to ask in the first place? Questions about his heavenly authority ("Where can you get this?") and his eternal identity ("Are you greater than our father Jacob?") — these were gaps in her knowledge that she didn't even know she'd had before she met this divine stranger at the well.

Had it been me, I think I would have played Jesus' cards differently. I mean, he knew what she needed to know and knew that she needed to know it. So I probably would have marched up to this woman and said, "Hello, my name is Jesus Christ. I am the Son of God and your Messiah. You may now dedicate your life to me so I can fill your thirsty soul with spiritual, living, eternal water."

Of course, had it been me, the story would likely have ended there! As the Heath brothers point out, we are too quick in simply downloading facts to others, when what they really need first is to *realize that they need these facts.* "The trick," the Heaths say, "to convincing people that they need our message, according to Loewenstein, is to first highlight some specific knowledge that they're missing. We can pose a question or puzzle that confronts people with a gap in their knowledge. We can point out that someone else knows something they don't."[5]

Now I don't mean to suggest that Jesus tricked the Woman at the Well into belief. Still, it does seem apparent that Jesus had a thorough knowledge of human nature, of our intense curiosity in the face of a mystery, and that he was comfortable *becoming* that mystery in order to reach this woman with the news of his soul-quenching, living water. Why would he do this? Well, the most obvious reason to me seems to be that he liked it.

God Loves a Mystery

I think, in this age of scientific discovery and intense theological study, that sometimes it's easy to overlook the truly mysterious aspect of God's eternal personality. I have to smile when I read the apostle Paul's writings in the New Testament, because even though he was arguably the world's first Christian theologian, he still thought Jesus was a never-ending mystery of deity and humanity. In his letter to the Colossians, Paul said his purpose was to help others "in order that they may know the mystery of God, namely, Christ,"[6] and he asked his readers to pray for him and his companions "so that we may proclaim the mystery of Christ."[7] In his first letter to the Corinthians, he readily admitted, "Now we see a dim reflection, as if we were looking into a mirror, but then [when Christ returns] we shall see clearly. Now I know only a part, but then I will know fully, as God has known me."[8]

At the same time, I often feel sad when I hear my fellow Christians today pontificate on their knowledge and understanding of the mysteries of God. Just recently my pastor preached a sermon on the Trinity — the theological idea that God is one person and at the same time is Father, Son, and Holy Spirit. During the sermon he made a statement that while the Trinity is true, it can never be fully understood in this lifetime.

Afterward a friend of mine casually belittled my pastor's statement, saying, "I've been studying the Bible for decades, and I understand everything there is to know about the Trinity."

My friend, it seems, has missed out on the breathtaking mystery of God and replaced it with her own limited understanding. I applaud her desire to study Scripture and to fill knowledge gaps as best she can, but I'm saddened that she doesn't understand that her studies now are simply cliffhangers in the mystery of eternity. Our God is not one who is easily explained or gently dissected into comfortable assumptions. If there is one thing I've learned, it's that God will not be defined or limited by our expectations.

God, it seems, loves a mystery.

If you don't believe me, just read his book, the Bible, to see what I mean. In Genesis 1 you'll find an eternal, self-existent, all-powerful being, someone in need of *absolutely nothing*. And yet, he created. He spoke and everything that exists was formed, from the awe-inspiring, mammoth sun that warms our solar system to the mitochondria that inhabit your very cells.

Why would God do that? He had no need. He was not, as we were taught in Sunday school, lonely or wishing for a friend. He needed no new hobbies — and he certainly could foresee the heartache and sinfulness that would run rampant in his creation over time. So why create at all?

It's a mystery.

In the book of Job you'll discover God making what appears to be a wager with Satan — a devastating bet that literally unleashes all hell into Job's life. Job had been a dedicated, righteous servant of God his entire life. Why would God orchestrate this kind of suffering for him? Job asked that question of God himself, and the answer he got was less than clear! In fact, when God was finished with him, Job's response was this: "Surely I spoke of things I did not understand, things too wonderful for me to know."⁹

Job's suffering? Also a mystery, even to the one who suffered it.

But perhaps the greatest mystery of all comes in Matthew 1,

where God inserted his very being within the uterus of a poor young woman who bore, not simply a son, but the actual Son of God. His love drove him to do that, you say, and of course you are right. But what of the height, the depth, the width, the expanse, the texture, and the heart of that love? Can that ever be understood? No, not in this life, and maybe not even in the next. Why?

It's a mystery.

And God, it seems, loves a good mystery. Continue reading the stories of Christ, and you'll discover him scattering seeds of the mysterious in just about everything he says and does: in his parables; in his sermons; in his confrontations with the religious elite; in his quiet moments with his followers; in his family; in his miraculous acts; in his death, burial, and resurrection; and more. It should be no surprise, then, that when God wanted to capture the attention of the Woman at the Well, he did what comes naturally with him. He spoke about a mystery — his mystery — and waited for her to respond.

"If you knew . . . who it is that asks you for a drink . . ."

In Life's Mysteries, We See Glimpses of God

I do not know all of God's reasoning behind the way he fills our lives with mystery. One thing I've learned, though, about Christ and his enigmatic ways is something that the Woman at the Well first discovered so many centuries ago.

In life's mysteries we see glimpses of God.

When Christ first hinted at his true nature and spoke a few clues about streams of living water, only then did the Woman at the Well begin to unravel the mystery of Jesus. "Are you greater than our father Jacob?" she asked. And when I read her words, I want to whisper in her ear, "Yes, now you're beginning to get it! Now you're on the right track!"

I have times in my life when I wish someone would whisper those words to me. I am so very good at forgetting to squint deeply into the mysteries that weave themselves into my life. Several years ago my husband, Mike, required unexpected surgery. Unfortunately the surgery solved one health problem but created another. While doctors were sorting this out, Mike was sick in bed. For months he was unable to work. The inflow of money dwindled while the flow of household and medical bills increased.

On top of it all, our old house was in serious need of painting. After getting several professional estimates (and laughing at the ludicrous idea that we'd be able to pay the painters), I gave up and began scraping the old paint off myself.

Why me? I grumbled to God. *And why Mike? He doesn't deserve this illness, and I certainly don't like being stuck out here in the blazing sun scraping flakes of paint off an old, beat-up house all by myself.*

But God didn't answer. Instead he left me to face the mystery in silence.

Four days later barely half of one side of the house was scraped (and that was one of the short sides of the house). It wasn't that our house was so big. It's just that it was a big job for only one person — namely, me!

Then on the fifth day, just after dinner, cars began to drive up to the house. Friends of ours from church piled out of their cars wearing old clothes and with scrapers in hand. Ladders were unloaded, cans of primer were opened, and within two hours the entire house was scraped and primer had been applied to all the exposed areas. Wow!

But that's not all. A few days later it was Saturday. A beautiful day when people should be boating at the lake, playing at a park, or hiking in the mountains. Instead cars again showed up at our house, and the painting began in earnest. These friends were so generous that they twice gave of their time for this chore. They even brought the paint, paintbrushes, and other supplies needed for the job. Then, just to rub it in, I guess, they gave us a gift of money they'd collected for us, to help out with the mounting tide of bills lying unpaid on my kitchen counter.

At the end of the day, brushes were washed out and tired muscles stretched, and everyone stood back to admire the house coated in new shades of blue.

What an incredible and tangible expression of love in the family of God! When one member was weak, others were strong. Our neighbors were amazed too. Who was this group of people that cheerfully laughed and joked while swinging paintbrushes all day? Why were they doing this? These questions opened the doors for us to tell our neighbors how Christ himself had motivated these wonderful friends of ours.

When Mike was sick in bed, when our family finances were strained to the breaking point, when the best I had to offer was simply much too little and much too late, I was living in one of God's mysteries. I can't say I really liked living that experience, but I can say that when all was said and done, I caught a glimpse of God in the laughing, friendly faces of our friends. I saw a shadow of Jesus in the sweaty, paint-splattered T-shirts they wore, and in the cool blue shade on the side of my house.

You see, it's often in the mysteries of life, in the moments and experiences that just seem to make no sense, that we, like the Woman at the Well, are treated to a little glimpse of heaven.

Eventually Mike's health improved enough for him to begin working again, and the story could end there, but there's one last bit to be told.

Nearly a year later I was looking through the papers my then school-aged son had brought home from a Bible class. There was a take-home handout called "Helping Hands," and on it the instructions read, "Write a way you might help others when you grow up." On this handout Tony had drawn a picture of himself painting a house the exact shades of blue his home now was, and he had written, "Help paint somebody's house."

Fast-forward about seven years or so, to when Tony was getting ready for high school. He had the opportunity to go on a short-term mission trip with the church youth group. He did the fund-raisers and went to all the training meetings. Got into a van and drove for a day and a half with a bunch of sweaty kids and devoted leaders. Slept on the floor of a school, gathered with other teens, sang songs to Jesus, held hands with other kids and prayed, and worked his heart out serving others.

Oh, yeah, one more thing.

Tony helped paint somebody's house.

I still remember standing beside my house, scraping infinitesimal flakes of paint, wiping sweat on my shirtsleeve, and complaining to God about how unfair and unkind he was being to me. I just didn't realize that God had cast me one of his glorious mysteries. I didn't understand that we would all catch a glimpse of Jesus as a result of this situation, or that it would be an image my son would remember — and seek to imitate — for years to come.

Oh, how I now wish that someone had taken me aside and whispered in my ear, "Hush now, Amy. Strangely enough, it all turns out well."

To be honest, I probably would have been skeptical, and it's likely I would have responded sarcastically and said, "Right, and how's that supposed to happen?" But I know what the answer would have been:

It's a mystery.

FOUR

facing the hidden reality

The woman said to him, "Sir, give me this water so that I won't get thirsty and have to keep coming here to draw water."

He told her, "Go, call your husband and come back."

"I have no husband," she replied.

—JOHN 4:15-17

She licked her lips before she realized she'd done it, and then quickly turned away.

It wouldn't be good to give away too many secrets. That had been a problem in the past. And besides, this Jew was a momentary interruption in her life. There was no reason to let him carry her confidences and then spread them like dung throughout his travels.

Only when she felt the mask was in place, when the expression on her face would no longer betray her, only then did she look back at the stranger.

So. Living water. Never thirst again. Hmm.

She wanted to slap herself when she felt her tongue roll over a crack in the corner of her mouth. She could see that he'd seen it too, that he knew she was really the thirsty one, even though he had been the one to ask for a drink. Well, when the truth comes out, the best thing to do is to turn it to your advantage. If this stranger really did have living water stored away somewhere, then she wanted it. After all, it was a big chore to have to lug her jar out to this well, day in and day out, refilling and carrying it back and forth from home over and over again. To never thirst again? That would be a miracle — and she could use a few miracles in her life.

The woman drew herself up confidently but assumed a more respectful air. "Sir," she said, "give me this water so that I won't have to keep coming here to draw water."

The stranger nodded approvingly and favored her with a gentle motion of acceptance.

A thought flashed through her mind, briefly, just after making her request. If this Jew really had living water that took away thirst forever, then why did he ask me to dip into the well to get a drink of water for him? But she shrugged the question away, at least for the time being. It was just another nagging secret she would keep to herself for later. The answer would come in time, and right now it was best to make this man believe that she believed because, well, because what if he did have living water after all? It was worth checking out.

Genuine enthusiasm seemed to fill his voice when he spoke next. "Go," he said, "call your husband and come back."

Inside her, the woman's stomach muscles clenched involuntarily at the sound of the request. This was a problem.

The man smiled her direction and then carefully placed his hands in his lap, waiting.

She started to turn away, caught sight of her water jar and turned back, felt herself begin to stammer, then took a deep breath. Blood rushed to her temples, and she worried that he could see her face flush, then figured that in this heat, the redness of her cheeks was unlikely to be noticed anyway.

She masked her face in nonchalance, noticing with surprise that her physical thirst was no longer pressing relentlessly at her senses but that the familiar thirst inside her soul had begun to call out within her again. She swallowed and then spoke with casual innocence, putting on her best air of truth while selecting a satisfying untruth to share. Finally she opted for half-truth, lofting it with practiced skill toward the mystery man before her.

"I have no husband," she said.

She hoped that would be enough.

"Go, call your husband and come back."

When Jesus said these seemingly innocuous words, I think the Woman at the Well must have grimaced inside. She knew her embarrassing reality of failed marriages and sexual immorality. Up to this point she'd been able to keep it safely hidden from this rabbi at Jacob's well. Now, however, this stranger was getting a little too close for comfort.

"Go, call your husband."

This was obviously more than a request. It was a challenge from the Son of God, a dare of sorts, asking this woman to admit the hidden reality that he already knew.

I wonder at her response sometimes. It seems that she would

have fit in well among today's spin doctors and masters of media manipulation! She had secrets, you see. In spite of her reputation at home, she saw no reason to spread that reputation among itinerant Jews passing through and drinking at her well. But she couldn't simply ignore the request. That would have been inappropriate and socially rude. So she chose to put a neutral spin on otherwise negative news.

"I have no husband," she said with feigned innocence.

Her answer masked well her failures in life. These four words offered the Christ a portion of the truth along with supposed protection of her status in this conversation with the man at the well. That carefully chosen language must have pleased her. After all, what difference would it make to this strange Jew? He would never know the reality of her situation, would he?

I have to admit I myself have been guilty of this kind of immature wordsmithery — in my prayers, in my conversations, even in my public speaking. We all have secrets, after all. We all have things that we'd simply rather not be known by others, or even by God. But, like this Woman at the Well, I've learned the hard way that Christ is not fooled by clever intent or cunning manipulation of facts. You cannot play hide-and-seek with God; you can only seek. And sometimes he uses that thing you are trying so hard to keep hidden as the catalyst to bring you out of your own darkness and into his light.

"Go, call your husband."

I read these words now, and I want to shake the Woman at the Well, to say plainly to her, "Don't miss this chance! It's a challenge for you to face reality, a plea from God for you to admit what he already knows: that you are not perfect. Here and now, he's graciously giving you an opportunity to come to him on your own terms. Don't make the mistake that we still make today, assuming we can cloud God's perception, cover our tracks, and paint ourselves in the best possible light."

But, of course, she wouldn't have listened any more than I listen to myself today. No matter what we do, we all have a little girl within us that childishly assumes we can hide our sins from everybody — sometimes in laughable ways. Just ask my sister Jody.

God Sees What We Would Keep Hidden

Jody Brolsma is a wonderful person and, in addition to being one of my dear sisters, she is also one of my best friends on this earth. She was also a bit of a stinker when we were kids!

"I was a typical snoopy little sister," Jody admits today. "Since I was at home when my brother and sisters were at school, I managed to explore their rooms and get into all kinds of trouble."

One afternoon Jody slipped into the room of one of our other sisters, Jill, to check out the toys that would eventually be hers (as the fourth of five children, Jody already knew what hand-me-downs were). Jill's Raggedy Ann doll was lying on the bed. "To this day I'm not sure what prompted me to do what came next," says Jody. At any rate she found our brother's fake vampire blood (another no-no) and used it to draw all over poor Raggedy Ann's face. "I remember holding the 'bleeding' doll, thinking, 'Someone's going to see this. I'd better hide it.'"

So Jody turned the doll face down on the pillow and left the scene of the crime.

Our dad was also the victim of Jody's afternoon explorations. We all knew that he kept a pack of Wrigley's Doublemint gum in his desk drawer. Chalk it up to budding creativity, but Jody carefully opened the package and the sticks of gum without tearing any of the wrappers, gently licked off the sugary coating on the gum, and made a neat row of teeth marks on each stick. Then she neatly rewrapped each stick and placed the package back in the drawer, certain that no one would find out.

Well, harsh reality never stays hidden for long. Jill came home and turned over her doll to find a gory mess. (Plus, Joel discovered that his fake vampire blood was missing, and Mom wasn't too happy to find that one of her nice pillowcases had been ruined.) Dad came home to enjoy a stick of gum and discovered a preschool art project instead. In both cases Jody's actions came to light and she, shall we say, *felt* the unhappy consequences. It was only a matter of time before she had to face — and ultimately admit — the reality of her failures.[1]

And that brings us back to the Woman at the Well. When Jesus tossed out that casual request, "Go, call your husband," it was so much more than the words that were spoken. It was a moment of truth. God himself was asking this parched woman if she was thirsty enough to come clean and admit that she had sins of which she was not proud. Her response shows that she wanted to avoid revealing the full reality of her lifestyle — and that she was childishly unaware that God easily sees what we would try so desperately to keep hidden.

In her desire to avoid judgment, she missed something else that I think is important here as well. She missed the reason behind God's challenge for her to admit her sin, the heart that saw more than what she'd been and dreamed of all she would be.

She didn't understand that God sees what we try to hide from him. And she could not yet grasp that God also sees what is kept hidden from us.

God Sees What Is Kept Hidden from Us

The awful truth — this woman's relational failures — had a correspondingly wonderful certainty that only God himself could see clearly: this woman's relational redemption. In the person of Christ all of heaven was suddenly, unexpectedly accessible. Reconciliation with God was literally within arm's reach of her, and that kind of reconciliation with righteousness would bear fruit of redemption within her human relationships as well.

This, I think, is one of the most overlooked aspects of the harsh reality that often comes with admitting our sins and weaknesses to God. We get so overwhelmed by the depth and breadth of our inability to truly live in harmony with God's expectations that we miss the fact that his commands aren't simply knuckle-down laws to blindly follow. They are sight for the blind, life and health for the sick, comfort and courage for the weary.

The call of God in our lives is, at its core, a challenge for us to trust that he alone sees all that is otherwise kept hidden from us in the physical realm, the emotional realm, the spiritual realm, the intellectual realm, and all the realms we have yet to learn or discover!

I think C. S. Lewis was a master at helping us glimpse this reality, and *I* first saw it in his finale to the Chronicles of Narnia series, *The Last Battle*. In this tale of a fantasyland, the forces of good and of evil face off in a cataclysmic battle at Lantern Waste. King Tirian of Narnia finds himself outnumbered and in dire straits, fighting near a wood outside a tiny stable. No one knows for sure what lies inside the stable, except that it appears to house a great evil that consumes anything that enters it.

Slowly but inevitably, the battle rages into night, and Tirian finds himself being forced backward toward the stable. Finally Tirian realizes that this battle is lost, and in a grand gesture, he grabs the leader of the enemy and falls backward toward death into the cursed stable. Once inside, his enemy is unexpectedly vanquished and Tirian is surprised to find himself among friends, in a place he never expected. I'll let C. S. Lewis describe it for you now:

> Tirian had thought — or he would have thought if he had had time to think at all — that they were inside a thatched stable, about twelve feet long and six feet wide. In reality, they stood on the grass, the deep blue sky was overhead, and the air which blew gently on their faces was that of a day in early summer. . . .
>
> "Fair Sir," said Tirian to the High King, "this is a great marvel. . . . Did I not come in out of the wood into the Stable? Whereas this seems to be a door leading from nowhere to nowhere." . . .
>
> Tirian put his eye to the hole [in the door]. At first he could see nothing but blackness. Then, as his eyes grew used to it, he saw the dull red glow of a bonfire

that was nearly going out. . . . So he knew that he was
looking out through the Stable door into the darkness
of Lantern Waste where he had fought his last battle. . . .
He looked round again and could hardly believe his
eyes. There was the blue sky overhead and grassy country spreading as far as he could see in every direction,
and his new friends all round him, laughing.

"It seems, then," said Tirian, smiling himself, "that
the Stable seen from within and the Stable seen from
without are two different places."

"Yes," said the Lord Digory. "Its inside is bigger than
its outside."

"Yes," said Queen Lucy. "In our world too, a Stable
once had something inside it that was bigger than our
whole world."[2]

Tirian expected to find death and horror inside that little
stable, but by the grace of God was instead welcomed into a world
of heavenly delights. Now, contrast Tirian's experience with that
of several self-absorbed, traitorous dwarves who had also been
in the battle. A group of them had been forced into the stable as
well. At first Tirian is reluctant to talk to them, but at the request
of Queen Lucy he relents. Imagine his surprise when he finds
them huddled into a small circle, listening intently as if they were
blinded by darkness. And, in fact, the dwarves are. As far as they
can tell, they are still trapped in a "pitch-black, poky, smelly little
hole of a stable."

"Are you blind?" Tirian asks incredulously.

"Can't you see?" adds Queen Lucy. "Look up! Look round!"
she says passionately. "Can't you see the sky and the trees and

the flowers? Can't you see *me*?"

The dwarves' response is heartbreaking in its stubbornness: "How in the name of all Humbug can I see what ain't there?" And so, despite the evidence to the otherwise, the dwarves continue to live in the darkness of their own minds, believing themselves to be prisoners in a stinky, filthy barn.[3] Their reality was heaven, but their experience was hell.

For the Woman at the Well, I'm certain that the world often felt to her like a "pitch-black, poky, smelly little hole of a stable." And like the dwarves in C. S. Lewis's tale, I'm guessing she never really expected it to get better; she was living a lifestyle of consequences that she deserved, after all. Yet here came Jesus, challenging, intruding on her self-built stable of despair.

"Can't you see?" the wind must have whispered. "This Jew is no ordinary man! Look up! Look around! Can you see the sky and the trees and the flowers? Can you see heaven in his eyes? Will you drink of his grace and forgiveness?"

At that moment, at that meeting beside an ancient well, Christ could see what was kept hidden from that desperate, thirsty woman. Like a wrangler gently entreating a wild horse, he cajoled her, called to her, intrigued her.

"Go, call your husband."

Would she take the bait? Would she take a step toward wholeness and admit what they both knew — that she was a sinner in need of God's grace? If she could see what God had seen, I think she would have gratefully, enthusiastically confessed everything right then and there. But sin kept those visions of her heavenly reality hidden from her, and so she held back, refusing to trust and instinctively trying to protect herself from yet another judgment against her.

God sees what is kept hidden from us, and if we don't yet trust his vision, then — like this woman — we reflexively resist his grace. And so we must understand one last thing before I can end this chapter about hidden things. We must know, you and I, one last truth that this Woman at the Well almost missed those many years ago. It is simply this: God hides each of us deep within his heart.

God Hides Us in His Heart

Why did Jesus keep this heavenly appointment by the well? Why did he patiently pursue this thirsty woman? Why did he persist in drawing her out, in helping her move from secret sin to public redemption? She certainly wasn't looking to meet God while doing her chores. She definitely wasn't ready to face a man who wanted to talk about her failings. She couldn't have imagined the heaven that Christ had planned for her to begin that day.

So why did he do it? Why take the time and effort and hardship to help a woman who resisted his help from the start? Why did he lead her gently, like a caring parent who wants his child to be the first to admit misbehavior, instead of confronting her with what he already knew of her sins? Why did he give her an opportunity to confess her moral failings rather than condemning her with a first-strike accusation?

I think the answer is found in the nature of God's love toward us. Listen to how the apostle Paul described it:

Who shall separate us from the love of Christ? Shall
trouble or hardship or persecution or famine or naked-
ness or danger or sword? . . .

No, in all these things we are more than conquer-
ors through him who loved us. For I am convinced
that neither death nor life, neither angels nor demons,
neither the present nor the future, nor any powers,
neither height nor depth, nor anything else in all
creation, will be able to separate us from the love of God
that is in Christ Jesus our Lord.[4]

Wow. Do you hear what that word is saying to you? It's simple,
really.

Jesus loves you.

Period.

Several years ago the Christian rock band Skillet released a
song titled, "Hey You, I Love Your Soul."[5] I am often reminded of
that song, because that congenial little phrase sums up the heart of
what I read in Paul's words and of what I am trying to communicate to you right now.

God *really* loves you.

So much so that Jesus was willing to enter your world, to live,
breathe, and die. To prove his eternal love for you by rising from the
dead and offering himself to you forever. When we made ourselves
the enemies of God, he still looked upon us with love because he
alone could see past the debris of a sinful life and into the beauty of
the heart he created. And he was willing to give all to help you see
it too. As Skillet says it in its song: "Love stretches out to die for its
enemies / Hey you, I love your soul."[6]

And here's the really good news: God is still in the business of loving souls, right now, today. Let me put that in more human terms.

It was during the 1980s when Mother Teresa decided to go to war. During this time of seemingly endless military conflict in Lebanon, heavy bombing had trapped thirty-seven special-needs children in a hospital deep inside the war-torn city of Beirut. Because the fighting still continued, no one was willing to risk an attempt to rescue the children. No one, that is, except Mother Teresa.

A frail-looking old woman, Mother Teresa stood only four feet, eleven inches tall and weighed less than one hundred pounds. But she was a small woman with great love, and she would not sit idly by while these children became just another story of the devastation of war. Motivated by love, she determined to let nothing stop her from saving those little ones — not bombs, not guns, and certainly not people telling her it was too risky. When she heard of the plight of the thirty-seven, she didn't hesitate. She was going to get those children and bring them to safety — no matter what.

"Impossible," they said. "You'll be killed!"

But Mother Teresa refused to believe them, and refused to back down.

"They are as good as dead," said some.

"Let them die," said others.

Mother Teresa's love for those unknown children overruled the advice of the supposedly wise, safe people. Instead of giving up those children for lost, she quickly flew to Beirut and immediately began making arrangements for the rescue. She informed everyone that she would go into the city the next day, "when the fighting stops." It was then she planned to bring out the children.

People looked at her in disbelief, possibly muttering "crazy" under their breaths. Love or no love, they knew there'd be no break in the fighting — it had been going on for months! And it seemed they were right. The fighting continued. Through the night. Into the morning, bullets and bombs raged until . . .

At precisely the time Mother Teresa had indicated, peace fell over the city. Guns were silent; bombs were held at bay. Unshaken despite the opposition to her loving rescue, Mother Teresa boarded an ambulance, drove deep into the war zone, and brought all thirty-seven children out of danger and into safety. Only after her work was finished did the fighting resume.[7]

My friend, this is the kind of tenacious love that Jesus lavishes on us — and that he lavished on the Woman at the Well. It's a love that goes into enemy territory — even into Samaritan land — to rescue brokenhearted little girls trapped by the warfare of sin that rages all around us.

Now, in recent days, some have tried to tell us that we must earn love, that others just aren't that into us, that we must settle for less than true love and be happy with any casual attention that masquerades as love instead.

Let me say this clearly: Those are not God's intentions toward you. He loves you as a father loves a precious child; he adores you as a mother who gains life and breath from her baby's laugh. He hides you in his heart like, well, like you are his very own child.

Before you finish this chapter, you must know that hidden truth and clutch it as close to your breast as you would warmth and hope. Like that Woman at the Well, you are so much more valuable than your society is telling you. You possess within you that beauty of soul that comes only from the hand of an infinite Artist. God smiles when he looks at you, because he alone can see the heart that reflects his creative light and genius.

When you are a wreck — physically, emotionally, and spiritually; when you find yourself an outcast with voices on all sides spreading gossip about your great failures and hurtful deeds; when you take a good look at yourself and realize the accusations are true, that you really are guilty as charged; when your worst accuser is the voice of your own conscience — then lift up your eyes. Like that Woman at the Well, catch a glimpse of Jesus' gaze. His eyes see who you are meant to be; his arms are open, ready to welcome your soul back into his healing presence.

When you hear your world (or your own voice) telling you something less than that, just smile and suggest that those thoughts go jump in a lake, because you know what your society finds unpopular to admit:

God hides you in his heart.

And that's what really matters.

speaking the truth

Jesus said to her, "You are right when you say you have no husband. The fact is, you have had five husbands, and the man you now have is not your husband. What you have just said is quite true."

"Sir," the woman said, "I can see that you are a prophet."

— JOHN 4:17-19

She inhaled and tasted the heat of midday in the back of her throat.

The stranger looked away for a moment, almost as if he were choosing carefully the next words he would speak. Did he just sigh?

She followed his gaze, looking back toward the town of Sychar. Her lips pressed together into a forced, tight smile. Back there they knew who she was. Back there they knew what she'd done. Back there they knew the truth about her failed marriages, her sexual immorality, and her sin-stained lifestyle.

She turned her eyes to the strange Jew and was slightly startled to catch him watching her. She dipped her head respectfully and waited. He was not long in responding.

"You are right when you say you have no husband," he said.

She felt a stab of panic slide through her.

"The fact is, you have had five husbands."

How could he know that? Had she given away a secret somewhere in their conversation? Did he make a lucky guess? Were there spies gushing their lies about her in the land of the Israelites?

Five husbands.

She felt sudden shame, like a woman caught in the very act of adultery. Like a young girl being used by an older man to fulfill his base desires. Like an old woman stripped and laid bare in front of a mocking crowd. Like a harlot preparing to face the righteous wrath of a mob carrying stones. And she had two disparate thoughts at the same time.

What have I done to myself?

How could he possibly know this about me?

"And the man you now have is not your husband."

She took the words like a blow. Her head sagged, and she lowered herself to one knee, leaning on the low wall of the well for both moral and physical support.

So he knew that, too.

He knew everything about her that she had wanted no one to know. Everything she'd ever done, this stranger could see as plainly as the sky above them. She blinked hard, willing herself to rise to her feet again. Sometimes the truth is easily hidden, especially from yourself, *she thought.* But even when it is hidden, it never truly goes away.

Obviously there was more to this stranger than met the eye. No average rabbi could have discerned these secrets about her, not in such detail and with such clarity. Only a holy man of God could read the secret knowledge of her past, of her sins, of her soul.

She waited for the condemnation to come. They both knew it was deserved; she only wondered whether he would curse her with only his words, or with words and actions both. Either way, she steeled herself for the judgment to come.

"What you have just said is quite true," he finished. And the tenor of his voice welled with love, not judgment. The words he spoke had force, but not heat. The passion of his confrontation was cloaked in the peace of his presence. Perhaps there would be no fire or brimstone, not today, at least. For some reason she felt an unexpected awe begin to fill the surroundings.

"Sir," she whispered across the dry space between them, "I can see that you are a prophet."

What do you do when it becomes apparent that a horrible truth about you is public knowledge? When you think you've hidden your secret so well, only to find out that this stranger standing before you knows all the intimate and embarrassing details of your life? I'm not sure how I would respond, but I actually admire this Woman at the Well for her measured, perceptive assessment of the rabbi who had just unleashed his bombshell upon her.

"Sir, I can see that you are a prophet."

Our female friend from long ago is now swimming in the deep end! The water is rising above her head, but she doesn't yet know whether to drink it deeply in or to hold her breath and hope it will wash over her. Yet I'm proud of her in a way, because at this revealing moment in the conversation, she didn't look behind her to see if someone was mouthing secrets behind her back, she didn't accuse Christ of trickery or deception, or even of being a first-class snoop into her personal life. Instead something within her spirit rightly identified the first glow of godhood within the man across from her. That godhood was still unclarified at this point — was he a prophet? A speaker for God to Samaria? Or the actual Christ? Who knew? But she did recognize the presence and activity of the Holy Spirit at that moment. Good for her! What she does with that fresh knowledge of deity nearby we'll explore more in the next chapter, but for now let it suffice that she began to understand that this was more than simply a conversation in the midday sun. It was a moment when eternity was touching temporality, a time when truth was going to make itself known whether she liked it or not.

There's a story about a man who conned his way into the orchestra of the emperor of China. Though the man had no musical talent, he faked his way through each practice, simply holding the flute in place and moving his fingers while the other musicians played. Because of his deception, he was paid well and lived comfortably.

Then the emperor requested a solo from each musician. The flutist panicked and pretended to be sick. Unfortunately the royal physician wasn't fooled. When the day came for the flutist to play his solo, he took poison and killed himself. This incident led to a phrase that we've all used: "He refused to face the music."[1]

And now, at last, it was time for the Woman at the Well to face the music. The question was, would the music make her dance, or make her cry?

Truth Hurts — and Heals

"The fact is, you have had five husbands, and the man you now have is not your husband."

I can't tell from these words whether Jesus was smiling or frowning when he said this to the Woman at the Well. There is no indication of whether he was angry or indifferent, passive or expressive, shouting or whispering. This is one of the many difficulties of Scripture: You can easily read what was said, but not so easily know *how* it was said. Regardless, the words are enough to make it clear that this "dirty laundry" was not what the woman expected to hear — nor what she wanted to hear. I think that hearing God himself speak plainly about her sin must have been an emotionally cauterizing experience.

Imagine the way it would burn within your heart if you looked God in the eyes while he said matter-of-factly, "Ah yes, you've committed adultery several times. And in fact you're having extramarital sex regularly with a guy right now, even though you know it's something I specifically told you not to do." Imagine how you'd feel hearing your mother or father, or your son or daughter, or anyone else important to you say those damning words.

But also imagine how this woman's life would have been woefully different if Christ had been unwilling to speak the truth to her at that moment. What if he had thought, *Oh well, I certainly don't want to make this woman uncomfortable. I might hurt her feelings, or I might offend her and make her dislike me.*

Worse yet, I might make her dislike herself, so I'd better hide the truth and pretend that everything is just fine. After all, I am Love, so certainly that means the truth can take a backseat to someone's feelings, right?

The absurdity of those kinds of thoughts is obvious when placed in the fictional mind of Christ. If Jesus will not tell us the truth, then how can he ever be trusted?

Yet that truth Jesus spoke was still a painful one. He might as well have said, "You are a moral failure. You, personally, have sinned and fallen short of the glory of God."

In this society at this time, divorce was frowned upon, but not terribly uncommon. In fact the standards in Jewish society indicated that a woman might be divorced twice or, on rare occasions, three times. For this woman to have been divorced five times — and to be currently cohabitating with a sixth man — was overwhelming evidence of her sexually immoral lifestyle.[2] Theologian Lawrence O. Richards has even speculated that she was not simply sexually immoral, but in fact Sychar's town prostitute.[3] And now this stranger at the well not only knew about her sinful secrets, he was unafraid to broadcast them directly to her face.

The truth hurts! It hurt when Jesus said it to that Woman at the Well, and it still hurts today because it reminds us of the many, many ways we repeatedly fall short of God's ideals for our lives.

Here's the secret, though. It's only by facing head-on the hurtful aspect of truth that we can come to experience the healing salve that truth carries within its very existence. A healing that goes beyond the simple physical or emotional experience of this life. Let me show you what I mean by telling you the true account of a girl named Kelly.

Kelly was a freshman at a large university, enjoying her first taste of adult life in the college environment. A pastor's kid, she now lived in an apartment with friends and generally spent her days in class and her nights hanging out with her friends and/or studying.

One evening, shortly after returning from a spring break trip back home, Kelly heard the doorbell ring at her apartment. When she opened the door, she was so surprised that she didn't know what to say. It was her father — and he didn't look happy.

"What are you doing here?" she finally stammered.

"I need to talk to you," her father said. "Can you come for a drive with me?"

Moments later the pair was in the parking lot of a small church, sitting under a streetlight in their car.

"I was cleaning out your car while you were home," Pastor Dad said, "and I found some things." He handed a picture to Kelly. "Honey," he continued, "is there anything in this picture that you think might break your father's heart?"

Kelly's heart froze, both with fear and anger. How dare he snoop around her stuff like that? How dare he accuse her of anything? She was an adult now, not his little girl anymore. She barely had to look at the picture to know what it was. It had been taken a few weeks prior, when she was at a party with friends. In one hand was a half-empty bottle of beer. In the other was a partially smoked cigarette. With one click of a camera, the truth about the secret party-girl life she'd been so careful to hide from her churchgoing parents had been exposed for all to see.

Finally she spoke through slitted lips. "Yes."

That was all she would say. Yes, there were things in this

picture that had broken her father's heart. Yes, she'd walked away from the Christian upbringing he'd spent eighteen years instilling in her. And no, now that the truth was known, she wasn't about to change for him or for anybody else.

Father and daughter sat in silence for a few moments, then he motioned toward the picture and said to her, "You take this. Go back to your apartment and put it up on your mirror. Every morning when you get up, look at it and ask yourself, 'Is this what God made me to be?'"

A little while later Kelly was back in her apartment, still smarting from the stinging truth that her father had confronted her with. Over the next few days, Kelly couldn't get two things out of her mind: the picture her father had found and the look of disappointment on her father's face. She'd been caught; she was living a lie, acting like a devoutly religious person around her parents and living out a party lifestyle when she was on campus. And now that her father knew, she could hide from the truth no longer.

It hurt Kelly to have her father face her with the truth. And it hurt Kelly to finally face the fact that her new lifestyle had disappointed not only her father but also her Father. That pain finally drove this young girl to her knees, where she poured out her heart to God, asking for his healing and forgiveness for her dishonest attitude toward both her friends and her parents.

A few days later, Kelly showed up at her father's house again. This time the meeting was different. Kelly confessed all, as she had done to God earlier, and asked her parents to forgive her for causing them pain. In the end that brief moment of truth in the church parking lot became a turning point for Kelly, both personally and in her relationship with her parents. Yes, it hurt to have her sins exposed. It hurt to have to face both her father and her heavenly Father with the truth of her dishonesty. But facing that truth also became the path to healing between Kelly and God, and between Kelly and her parents.[4]

Truth Has Consequences

Make no mistake, though. Even though all worked out well for Kelly and her parents, truth has serious consequences, especially in relation to Christ. Thomas Hauker is proof of that.

It was in 1555 that Thomas Hauker was sentenced to die, to be burned at the stake for his dogged refusal to deny the truth about his Christian faith. The night before his execution, a friend visited Hauker's jail cell.

"I must know the truth," the man said earnestly. Thomas gazed into his friend's eyes and saw the hunger, the desperate need behind those words. It was ironic, really. After all, given his impending death, Thomas should've been asking for favors from his friend, not vice versa. Tomorrow he would be led to the top of a mountain of wood, bound to a stake at its center, then callously lit on fire to burn in agony until he was dead, dead, dead.

Yet at the end Thomas asked for no favors. And he found himself facing a friend who spoke with grave urgency.

"Thomas," the friend whispered, "I have to ask you this favor. I *need* to know if what the others say about the grace of God is true. Tomorrow, when they burn you at the stake, if the pain is tolerable and your mind is still at peace, lift your hands above your head. Do it right before you die." The friend looked sorrowfully into Thomas's eyes, paused a moment, then spoke one last time. "Thomas," he said, "I *have* to know."

Thomas Hauker spoke gently, reassuring his friend and promising to reveal whether or not God's grace was still true even in the worst of life's circumstances, even while burning at that stake.

Next morning, the martyr was led to his fiery destination. The flames were kindled, then raged, ravaging the man who refused to bow to any but Christ. In the heat of it all, Thomas Hauker's body sagged, slowly being consumed by the merciless heat. At last his skin was burnt to a crisp, his fingers were gone, and most in the crowd assumed the man was finally dead.

But those who turned away then missed the most miraculous sight. Suddenly the "dead" man stirred. In silence he raised his still-burning hands high over what was left of his head. He clapped those hands together. Once. Twice. Three times. Then, at last, his arms fell to his sides, and he moved no more.

The crowd was silent at first, and then moments later joined Thomas Hauker in thunderous applause and praise for God. For just before he died, the martyr had testified one last time to the truth, the *Truth*, of God.[5]

Thomas Hauker's dedication to truth cost him, horrifyingly, his life. The pain he experienced is something I can imagine only in my nightmares. And yet, if his own testimony is to be believed, his unwillingness to waver from the truth of eternity also brought about an awe-inspiring consequence of courage and fortitude, in the moment of his greatest agony, to experience the soul-healing mercy of God. His heartbreakingly beautiful example still stands, hundreds of years later, as evidence of powerful consequences — both good and bad — of coming face-to-face with the truth of this life and the life to come.

I know that when Jesus confronted the Woman at the Well with the truth about her sins, she must have been worried about the consequences of that exposure. This man with whom she spoke was a hated Jew, and a rabbi at that. Would he harm her, perhaps even incite his disciples to stone her to death for her infidelities? Would he curse her? Would he despise and reject her, the way so many others had?

"The truth is incontrovertible," Winston Churchill once said. "Ignorance may attack it and malice may deride it, but in the end, there it is."[6]

Newscaster Katie Couric and CBS learned this the hard way in the fall of 2006. At that time the big news was that Ms. Couric was leaving her cushy position as host of the *Today* show to take a similarly cushy position with a network rival as anchor for *CBS Evening News*. In promoting its new anchor, CBS released a picture of Katie Couric looking svelte and lovely as ever. Problem was, that picture had previously been used, and in the original, Katie had been about twenty-five pounds heavier! Turns out the network decision makers had doctored Ms. Couric's press photo to make her look slimmer and more attractive, apparently assuming that no one would be able to tell the difference. But in the Internet age, Katie's photo-fictional weight loss was soon the stuff of legend, showing up on blogs and news sites all over the world. The truth was out there — and it wasn't pretty. The public relations fallout was a media disaster for both Katie Couric and CBS.[7]

Likewise the consequences of Jesus' exposure of the truth about the Woman at the Well had the potential to be a relational disaster — but Jesus apparently had other things in mind. In fact the first consequence of his actions seems to have been the woman's realization that Jesus was more than just a man.

"Sir," she said, "I can see that you are a prophet."

Now there were two truths that had to be dealt with. First was the truth of her sinful situation. Second, and infinitely more important, was the truth that Jesus was something extraordinary. The stakes had been immeasurably raised, and it was time for her to piece together the true nature and identity of the man who stood before her.

Jesus Is Truth

The interesting thing about Jesus is that he makes no apologies. Nowhere in Scripture do you find him saying he is sorry for speaking the truth. In fact just the opposite! So much so that in John 14:6, the apostle recorded Jesus as saying, "I am the way and *the truth* and the life" (italics mine). When the Woman at the Well finally began to recognize Christ's true identity, it was not simply because he spoke the truth; it was because he *is* the truth. Or as Winston Churchill might have said, "There *he* is!"

Now then, what do you do when confronted by that kind of truth? That was the question that the Woman at the Well had to answer on a moment's notice. Those of us who have come after her have at least had more time to consider this Truth that seeks to know and be known by us. And yet that doesn't make it any easier. Consider the experience of Zahea (pronounced Zuh-HAY-ya) Hassen.

"There is only one God, and Mohammed is his prophet," Zahea's grandfather used to repeat to her. These words of her *jiddee* rang in her ears as she paged her way through a Bible given to her by a friend. "That is what the Islamic Druze religion believes," he had said. "You were born a Druze, Zahea, and you will always be a Druze."

Growing up as a child of Lebanese immigrants to America, Zahea knew she was supposed to be Druze, but something inside her balked at that idea. Deep within she hungered for God, hungered for truth, hungered so much that it gnawed at her soul.

Why are there so many religions? she questioned. *Are they all right? Which religion is true?*

So now this gifted high-school sophomore had decided to find out, launching her own personal study of the world's major religions. Long ago she had come to the conclusion that there must be one, and only one, absolutely correct manner in which to be reconciled to God. Now she was determined to find that way. To find the truth.

She turned another page in the Bible and read about Jesus, about how he came to earth to reconcile people to God, about how he paid the penalty for sin through his execution on a cross, and about how he defeated death once and for all by rising from the dead.

Was this the truth? She had to find out. Zahea's father had a friend who was a pastor in her hometown, so Zahea turned to that friend and begged to hear more. Reverend Frank Baugh fascinated this sixteen-year-old with his answers to her questions and his stories of Jesus. Zahea's hunger grew.

At that point she began to read the Bible voraciously. Two

Scriptures leaped from the page and planted themselves in her heart. John 3:16, which read in her old English version of the Bible, "For God so loved the world, that he gave his only begotten Son, that whosoever believeth in him should not perish, but have everlasting life" (KJV). Also Acts 16:31, which read, "Believe on the Lord Jesus Christ, and thou shalt be saved, and thy house" (KJV).

Zahea was torn. Here, she believed, was the truth. Jesus. Not Mohammed, not the Druze religion, not the Koran. Jesus was the true way to God. Yet she remembered the words of her grandfather, "You were born a Druze, Zahea, and you will always be a Druze."

The pressure was almost too much to bear. How could she, a mere teenager, reject the religion of her ancestors in favor of Christianity, in favor of Christ?

Maybe I can be a "closet Christian," Zahea thought one private night in 1950. *Maybe I can believe in Jesus inside, but follow Islam's ways outside.*

Just then another Scripture came to her mind from the book of Joshua: "Choose you this day whom ye will serve . . . but as for me and my house, we will serve the LORD" (Joshua 24:1,5 KJV).

Zahea reports that, at that moment, the Scripture "seared both my brain and my heart. Obediently I knelt down, repented, confessed my sins, and accepted Jesus Christ into my heart." The next day she told her family that she was a Christian and wanted to be baptized. Her parents reminded her that she was born a Druze, always would be a Druze, and could not be a Christian. Zahea continued to affirm that she was indeed a Christian and that she wanted to be baptized. Her parents told her she would have to wait until she was eighteen, when she would be a legal adult.

Risking severe disapproval, she went public with her newfound faith, telling anyone who would listen that Jesus is the only way to God.

Thankfully her family did not renounce their Christian daughter, and many listened to what she had to say. Years later Zahea was instrumental in leading members of her family, and her own children, into a relationship with Jesus.

For that, many people are grateful — especially me. You see, a few years after becoming a Christian, Zahea married, taking her husband's last name of Nappa. A few years after that she had one very special son who, at the age of sixteen, also became a Christian. Then in 1986, when he was twenty-two, that Christian young man, Mike Nappa, became my husband. By the grace of God we've been happily married ever since.[8]

I wonder sometimes how my life would have been different if Christ had not confronted Mike's mother with the truth. I wonder what might have happened if the Woman at the Well had been spared the truth as well.

And I wonder what will happen if you, dear sister, turn away from the truth of Christ. If it hurts you so much that you try to run away from his healing.

Let's not find out, okay?

removing the distractions

"Our fathers worshiped on this mountain, but you Jews claim that the place where we must worship is in Jerusalem."

Jesus declared, "Believe me, woman, a time is coming when you will worship the Father neither on this mountain nor in Jerusalem. You Samaritans worship what you do not know; we worship what we do know, for salvation is from the Jews. Yet a time is coming and has now come when the true worshipers will worship the Father in spirit and truth, for they are the kind of worshipers the Father seeks. God is spirit, and his worshipers must worship in spirit and in truth."

— JOHN 4:20-24

Her mind raced with a million worries; her heart rushed through the microseconds between its normal beats, like a musician just slightly ahead of the music.

So he was a prophet, then. That certainly explained a few things — but not enough things. And it gave her no clue as to what kind of prophet this Jewish stranger might be. Was he one of the ones who punished sin or simply railed against it?

At the same time, his words, though hurtful, had been like a salve applied to the soul. Stinging with truth, but also dripping with love. A messy, revitalizing rainstorm of harshness and healing that her thirsty soul was drawn to like, well, like a woman to a well.

She couldn't leave, she decided. Not now. Not without learning more of this absurdist prophet. But prophet or no, it was dangerous to let this conversation continue along this course.

"Our fathers worshiped on this mountain," she said abruptly, and she was surprised at first to hear a veiled challenge in her voice. Then she remembered that he was, after all, a Jew, and those hypocrites from Israel had given her and her people nothing but grief, even daring to condemn their worship of the one true God. "But you Jews claim that the place where we must worship is in Jerusalem — "

"Believe me, woman," the prophet declared. "A time is coming when you will worship the Father neither on this mountain nor in Jerusalem."

She almost jumped at the forcefulness of his interruption. Was the prophet angry now? Had she crossed a theological line with her implied accusations against his people? No, the timbre of his speech still communicated peace, almost friendship. He was impassioned, but not inflamed.

"You Samaritans worship what you do not know," he was saying now. "We worship what we do know, for salvation is from the Jews."

A new sensation began to warm the woman, and it was a warmth that actually cooled the heat her skin felt from the sun beating down above her. At this moment, in this time, she unexpectedly realized that this rabbi/prophet/Jew was treating her not as just a stupid, unclean Samaritan woman. He was speaking to her as a teacher does a student, as a master does his disciples, placing her on equal footing with any follower of God, male or female alike.

She felt herself blushing again, this time with pleasure instead of shame. She hung on his words, trying to make sense of the new, eternal truths that he was spilling out to her. But he spoke so quickly, laying out the complex secrets of heaven with authority and obvious understanding. And she was only a child, trying hard to pick up the message of words that formed thoughts foreign and confusing to her experience.

"Yet a time is coming," he continued, "and has now come when the true worshipers will worship the Father in spirit and in truth, for they are the kind of worshipers that the Father seeks. God is spirit, and his worshipers must worship in spirit and in truth."

When she was a young girl, she'd once been so thirsty that she'd happily poured a whole bucket of water over her face and was surprised to find that, when the bucket was empty, the bulk of the water she wanted had escaped her thirsty tongue and splashed all around her instead. The experience had left her breathless and gasping for more of the liquid of life. She felt like that little girl again at this very moment; like this prophet had, by barely trying, opened a flood of living truth that had splashed around her in tantalizingly close fashion — but still left her thirsty, oh, so thirsty, for more.

So many truths that she longed to understand but that were so difficult to grasp had just spilled from this stranger's lips. And he spoke of the Father God with an intimacy and confidence that *was both shocking and confusing, as if God were more than God to him, but actually his living, breathing Father.*

How could that be? And what did it all mean? For the first time in this meeting at the well, she didn't know what to say.

The theology recorded in John 4:20-24 is breathtaking, and its implications enormous. God himself has just revealed several foundational truths about eternity, spoken them casually and with authority, to a congregation of one. If we pay attention to Jesus' short comments here, we — along with the Woman at the Well — discover that,

- God can be known (verse 22).
- The Jewish people are God's chosen instrument for bringing salvation (Jesus Christ himself) to the world (verse 22).
- There's a difference between true and false worship (verse 23).
- God seeks worshipers — true worshipers (verse 23).
- God is spirit (verse 24).
- Location is irrelevant when it comes to worshiping the omnipresent God (verse 21).
- Truth and spirit-being are essential to the worship of God (verse 24).

The theology of any one of those implications above would be enough to fill several volumes of academic textbooks and seminary shelves. But while I'm intrigued by the theology in this portion of our story, I find myself much more attracted to the humanity enveloped within it. The Woman at the Well was no theologian, but given her approach to Jesus, she might have been a good politician!

Up to this point the conversation with Christ had been unexpected and disorienting, but then Jesus laid out the truth to her in no uncertain terms: "You have had five husbands, and the man you have now is not your husband."

You can almost see this dear woman begin to squirm under the spotlight of heaven's hero. She can't simply run away, not now, not yet. After all, as we noted in the last chapter, she has just unmasked the first mystery of Christ: "I can see that you are a prophet," she said to him. But how to deal with that pesky issue of sin that he so easily exposed? The woman's next response would make rhetoricians and debate coaches proud as peacocks, as in one simple sentence she throws a one-two punch of verbal jousting back into the face of Jesus.

First she adopts the thoroughly modern sentiment, "When you can't deny it, avoid it altogether," and charges forward to *change the subject.* As theologian Lawrence O. Richards explains it, "She [the Woman at the Well] tried to avoid the issue of sin by raising a theological question."[1]

Propaganda scholars and logic educators call this evasive maneuver an error of faulty logic where "someone sidesteps an issue by changing the topic."[2] Notice she doesn't deny Christ's accusation of her infidelities, but she also pointedly does not acknowledge it. Instead it's as if she has breezily waved her hand at a cocktail party and said, "But enough about me. I see that you're a prophet, so let's talk theology for a bit, shall we?"

It also appears that our demure mistress was just beginning to employ the propaganda technique of card stacking (omitting key thoughts and/or facts in order to bolster your position and slant the conversation in your preferred direction).[3] When confronted with her own sin, she began to try to redefine the topic of conversation so that it was not about her failings but about the error of the Jews in their insistence that Jerusalem be the center of worship.

I would love to smile knowingly at this point and say to you, "See how foolish she was! She was talking with the Son of God and thought a flawed rhetorical technique that's used for manipulating others' perceptions would actually turn this conversation in her favor. *Tsk tsk*, what a childish thing to do. I'm so glad we're not like that today."

But, of course, if you know me at all (and I think you do), you know that I am guilty of this same kind of flawed approach to life every day, both in my relationship with God and in my relationships with others. Fortunately, as Nora Ephron so eloquently reminded me, I am not alone.

Pay No Attention to the Me Behind the Curtain

Recently I enjoyed the wry humor and sensitive writing of Ephron's book *I Feel Bad About My Neck.* In this collection of essays about womanhood, Ephron laughingly and lovingly points out one of the unsightly hazards of growing up: Eventually you get an older woman's neck.

Oh, the necks. There are chicken necks. There are turkey gobbler necks. There are elephant necks. There are necks with wattles and necks with creases that are on the verge of becoming wattles. There are scrawny necks and fat necks, loose necks, crepey necks, banded necks, wrinkled necks, stringy necks, saggy necks, flabby necks, mottled necks. There are necks that are an amazing combination of all of the above.[4]

And so, according to Ephron, when she and her neck-weary friends go out on the town, they do what any self-respecting woman does—and what our dear Woman at the Well tried to do. They avoid the subject. They deliberately draw attention away from the neck and hope others will be polite enough not to notice. They stack the deck (figuratively speaking) with other topics of conversation. As she reveals, "Sometimes we go out to lunch and I look around and realize we're all wearing turtleneck sweaters. Sometimes, instead, we're all wearing scarves, like Katharine Hepburn in *On Golden Pond*. Sometimes we're all wearing mandarin collars and look like a white ladies' version of the Joy Luck Club. It's sort of funny, and it's sort of sad."[5]

What is it about us women that makes us feel so adamant about hiding what we know everyone else can already see for themselves? Wearing a turtleneck certainly doesn't change the fact that I am a middle-aged woman in my forties. And debating tidbits of theology doesn't disguise from God the sin that is so obvious in my life. I don't know about you, but often when I approach God—be it on Sunday morning at church or some weeknight when I am alone in prayer—I feel like the erstwhile Oscar Zoroaster Phadrig Issac Norman Henkle Emmanuel

Ambroise Diggs. Of course, you perhaps know him better as L. Frank Baum's wonderful Wizard of Oz.[6]

A classic scene from the film version of Baum's book is a perfect picture of what I think goes on between God and me — and what I think happened (to some extent) with the Woman at the Well and Jesus. Near the end of the movie, Dorothy and her companions have finally defeated the Wicked Witch of the West. Now they come to the throne room of the Wizard of Oz to ask their favors once more (a heart for the Tin Man, a brain for the Scarecrow, and so on).

Thunder sounds, lights flash. A huge and imposing holographic image of the Wizard displays itself before the travelers, flames bursting high and smoke billowing all around as the Wizard's voice explodes through the room. Dorothy and her friends literally tremble where they stand, awed by the impressive image before them. Then, at a key moment, Dorothy's little dog, Toto, noses over to a green drapery in a corner of the room. Unobserved at first, Toto pulls away the curtain to reveal the truth: The "great and powerful Oz" is nothing more than a con man using sound effects and theatrics to make himself appear to be much more than he really is.

"Pay no attention to that man behind the curtain!" the image bellows in futility when Dorothy first discovers the deception. But, of course, once the shade has been removed, nothing can distract Dorothy from the truth. The so-called Wizard of Oz is just faking his way through life, hoping that the flash and spectacle of his machinations will divert attention from the fact that he's a fraud.[7]

There was no lightning or thunder during the Woman at the Well's conversation with Jesus, but there was a curtain that she tried to pull closed, a covering that she hoped would divert Christ's attention from the fact that she was a fraud, a thirsty woman living a life of deception. When confronted with the truth about her sinfulness, her immediate reflex was to hide the truth, to change the subject, to ignore the problem and hope it would simply go away.

"This woman, like many of us," says Donna Lamb, "had mastered the art of spending endless hours in discussions, making long arguments in which she could completely hide her true feelings."[8]

Wow, that sounds so much like me I almost hated to quote it in this book! But it's no secret that I am far from perfect, that I have failed God's standards again and again. Still, when I lash out at my husband, or when I'm tempted to shirk my work, or when my compassion tanks just feel so empty that I don't even care that children are starving in Africa, or when I act in ways at work or home or anywhere that simply give Christ's reputation a smear of sin, something inside me still peeks heavenward and says, "Pay no attention to the me behind the curtain, God. Let's ignore my sins today and maybe they'll just go away. Instead let's talk about something else."

Funny thing is that often God will let me change the subject temporarily. But one thing I have learned is that he never lets me avoid the truth — or its consequences — for long. Let me show you what I mean.

God Doesn't Have Attention Deficit Disorder

Dory, in the hit animated movie *Finding Nemo*, is one of the most humorous cartoon characters ever created. If you happen to have lived on the moon for the last several years and are unfamiliar with this Pixar classic, the basic story is this: Marlin is a clown fish living in the ocean. One day his son, Nemo, is captured by a scuba diver and taken away in a white boat. The rest of the film follows Marlin's globe-spanning attempt to rescue his son.

Along the way Marlin teams up with Dory, a blue tang fish with short-term memory problems. As a result Dory is easily distracted by anything and anyone that she happens to discover. At a key moment during the movie, Marlin and Dory find themselves at the opening of a large, undersea trench. Just moments ago Dory was given a stern warning: "When you come to this trench, swim through it, not over it." Now she and Marlin face the trench, and Marlin decides the best route would be to swim over it. Dory can't remember why, but she says:

"Something's telling me we should swim through it, not over it."

"Are you even looking at this thing?" Marlin says. "It's got death written all over it!"

"I really, really think we should swim through."

Unconvinced, Marlin plays the same diversion game that the Woman at the Well tried with Christ. "Look!" he says suddenly, pointing over Dory's shoulder. "Something shiny!"

"Where?" shouts Dory in excitement, completely distracted from her original point.

"Oh, it just swam over the trench!" says Marlin. "Come on, we'll follow it!"

And poor little attention-deficit Dory? She gleefully says, "Okay!" and they both head toward the top of the trench where nothing but danger awaits.[9]

Sometimes it seems like we are foolish enough to think that God is like that little blue tang fish in *Finding Nemo*. As long as we distract his attention ("Oh God, please care for orphans in Asia!"), he will forget the important message he was trying to communicate to us and we'll get to do whatever it was that we wanted to do in the first place. But God doesn't play that kind of game; he doesn't have ADD, and he won't let his purpose be delayed for long.

When the Woman at the Well slipped into evasive mode and tried to distract Jesus from her sin by bringing up a discussion of the sins of the Jews, I think it's interesting to note Jesus' immediate response. First (although admittedly this is conjecture on my part), it appears to me that he cut short the woman's comments—that he didn't let her finish whatever it was she'd started to say.

Her statement, "Our fathers worshiped on this mountain, but you Jews claim that the place where we must worship is in Jerusalem," appears to be an introductory thought at best. It's a simple statement of fact as an initiator of topic. Try saying a similarly fashioned fact-phrase to a friend sometime: "My father is from the northernmost part of Ireland." "My car is a Ford Escort." "My church tells me I should go to India on a mission trip." I can almost guarantee that the response you'll get will be, "And . . . ?" That's because this kind of prefatory statement almost always comes just before an application of, or question about, that statement of fact. It's a common conversational and debate structure that appears to have been interrupted before the second part of the structure could be completed.

From what I can tell, this woman had more to say, maybe a favorite argument that she carried around for dealing with intrusive religious folk, maybe a sincere question about the place of worship within geographical lines. But it seems obvious she was just getting started on her attempt to divert Jesus' attention away from her — and that Jesus cut short her juvenile attempts at debate and evasion.

Second, it's interesting to note how, in recording this event, the apostle John set apart the way Christ spoke his response to her at this juncture of the conversation: "Jesus *declared* . . ." (verse 21, italics mine).

Up to this point John has recorded Jesus' words with common, ordinary conversation markers such as "Jesus said" and "Jesus answered." Even Christ's stunning declaration that the woman was an adulterer was prefaced simply by this mild statement: "Jesus said to her . . ."

Now, however, something has changed; there's a new dynamic emerging in the conversation. Instead of simply speaking truth, John abruptly described Jesus as suddenly "declaring" truth — an unexpected emphasis that shows up only once more in this historical script (in verse 26, when John indicated that Jesus "declared" that he is indeed the Messiah).

As I said earlier, I can almost see the woman squirming under the unwavering gaze of Jesus. Her intent at this moment seems to be, first and foremost, to shine the spotlight of his attention on a comfortable target — say, on a theological debate or the sins of his society. Look at the words she uses in her comment (italics mine):

"*Our fathers* worshiped on this mountain, but *you Jews* claim that the place where *we* must worship is in Jerusalem."

Suddenly she's not talking about herself anymore. Now the topic of conversation is "our fathers" and "you Jews" and "we" Samaritans as a general population. All comfortable, ambiguous groups of people who are related to, but safely removed from, one single woman guilty of many, many sins. Will Jesus take the bait? To be sure, he doesn't leave her with faulty theological knowledge, and he easily addresses her concerns about culture and worship of God. But does he let her move away from the personal, individual accountability with which this conversation started? Let's look at his first response (italics mine):

"Believe me, *woman*, a time is coming when *you* will worship the Father neither on this mountain nor in Jerusalem."

She's talking in generalities; Christ comes back with specifics, addressing her personally as "woman" and telling her point-blank, "*you* will worship the Father." Only after he has clearly identified her as an individual right up front does he then allow her to see herself in the larger group of worshipers that the Father seeks. And that's not all . . .

I remember when I was first learning how to use a typewriter, I practiced by typing over and over the phrase: "Now is the time for all good men to come to the aid of their country." When I got bored, I would sometimes shorten it to simply a repeated statement of the opening: "Now is the time Now is the time Now is the time."

In verse 23 of John 4, Jesus is recorded as saying pretty much the same thing to that Woman at the Well. "A time is coming," he said, "and *has now come* when the true worshipers will worship the Father in spirit and truth" (italics mine).

Do you see what he was telling her? What he was calling her

to understand? Let's put it together a little differently:

"Believe me, woman . . ."

"A time is coming when you will worship the Father . . ."

"A time . . . has now come . . ."

Or, in the Amy Nappa paraphrase: *Now is the time for all thirsty women to come to the living waters of worshiping the Father.*

Jesus looked directly into the eyes of the Woman at the Well, and though he allowed her some freedom to roam in this conversation, he refused to let her miss out on what it was that he'd brought to give. She had God's attention, and when God unmistakably looks your way, it's always best to respond.

Pay Attention to God's Attention

To put it another way, we need to learn to *pay attention to God's attention.*

A few thousand years ago a thirsty, hurting woman thought she was all alone in the world. She spent her days going through the motions of existence and her nights in the silence of social isolation. She was an unnoticed blip in the grand scheme of the cosmos, or at least we would have expected her to be. But one unbelievable day she caught God's eye; she was suddenly the focus of God's undivided attention. And when you have God's attention, it's best to pay attention — and respond in kind.

The apostle Paul learned this the hard way during a trip to Damascus. I'll let him tell you that story for himself (repeating what he once said during a trial before Roman appointee King Agrippa):

"King Agrippa, I am very blessed to stand before you and will answer all the charges the evil people make against me. You know so much about all the customs and the things they argue about, so please listen to me patiently.

"All my people know about my whole life, how I lived from the beginning in my own country and later in Jerusalem. They have known me for a long time. If they want to, they can tell you that I was a good Pharisee. And the Pharisees obey the laws of my tradition more carefully than any other group. . . .

"I, too, thought I ought to do many things against Jesus from Nazareth. And that is what I did in Jerusalem. The leading priests gave me the power to put many of God's people in jail, and when they were being killed, I agreed it was a good thing. In every synagogue, I often punished them and tried to make them speak against Jesus. I was so angry against them I even went to other cities to find them and punish them.

"One time the leading priests gave me permission and the power to go to Damascus. On the way there, at noon, I saw a light from heaven. It was brighter than the sun and flashed all around me and those who were traveling with me. We all fell to the ground. Then I heard a voice speaking to me in the Hebrew language, saying, 'Saul, Saul, why are you persecuting me? You are only hurting yourself by fighting me.'

"I said, 'Who are you, Lord?'

"The Lord said, 'I am Jesus, the one you are persecuting. Stand up! I have chosen you to be my servant and my witness — you will tell people the things that you have seen and the things that I will show you. This is why I have come to you today. I will keep you safe from your own people and also from the others. I am sending you to them to open their eyes so that they may turn away from darkness to the light, away from the power of Satan and to God. Then their sins can be forgiven, and they can have a place with those people who have been made holy by believing in me.'

"King Agrippa, after I had this vision from heaven, I obeyed it. I began telling people that they should change their hearts and lives and turn to God and do things to show they really had changed. I told this first to those in Damascus, then in Jerusalem, and in every part of Judea, and also to the other people."[10]

When the time was right, Jesus — literally — shined a light on Paul just as bright as the one he shined on the soul of the Woman at the Well. And like he did with the Woman at the Well, Jesus patiently and unapologetically confronted that man with the truth of his sins.

I love Paul's dumbfounded response: "Who are you, Lord?" Paul had no idea exactly who it was that was tearing up his carefully constructed theology and lifestyle of Pharisaical sinfulness. Yet whoever it was, Paul knew he had to be "Lord."

For one unforgettable moment of human history, Paul was at the epicenter of God's attention. When that happened, Paul made sure to pay attention to God's attention!

The result? "After I had this vision from heaven," Paul declared, "I obeyed it."

Ron Belsterling and his youth group choir also learned this important lesson that Paul learned. Listen to how my friend Rick Lawrence tells that story:

Not long ago I was talking with Ron Belsterling, an associate professor of Christian Education at Nyack College in New York, about an experience he had as he was pursuing his doctoral degree — it had profoundly sealed his perspective on the power of Jesus-centered mentoring. As part of a doctoral project, Ron had convinced a church to experiment with an outreach trip that targeted a nearby inner-city neighborhood instead of the youth group's traditional overseas trip that included four days of "ministry" and six days of fun on the beach. Parents who were fine about their kids going on a cross-cultural mission/fun trip were very worried about them walking the streets of an urban neighborhood that was just 20 minutes away.

One night Ron and the kids on his inner-city outreach looked out the window of their hotel and saw two men viciously kicking a woman who was high on drugs, and therefore unable to defend herself or run away. Ron turned to these protected, wide-eyed middle-class kids and asked, "What are we going to do about this?"

The kids said, "Well, we can't go down there!"

Ron answered, "Why not? *Down there* is where Jesus would be."

The kids responded: "What can we do? The only thing we know how to do is sing!" (Most of the kids on the outreach were part of the church's respected youth choir.)

Ron fired back, "Well, let's go down there and sing then. We'll give what Jesus has given us to give."

So the whole group trouped down to the street, stood on the opposite sidewalk, and started singing. The two guys kicking the woman looked up, startled, then immediately ran away in fear. The woman then crawled across the street and lay down in the middle of the kids as they continued singing.[11]

Ron felt certain that God cared about what was happening in this inner-city neighborhood — that God's attention was focused on those people who, like the Woman at the Well, were struggling to overcome the grip of sin and isolation in their lives. He felt this so much that he took his entire youth group to that place, and while they were there, God showed them a woman about whom he cared deeply — drug addict or no. When Ron and those kids saw God's child being abused in the street, they chose to pay attention to God's attention, to do something, anything, in response to God's attention. The results were beautiful.

I wonder how my life would be different if I could truly learn the same lessons that Paul and Ron learned. It is so easy for me to whimper, "Pay no attention to the me behind the curtain," to foolishly wish that God might have ADD today and, for once, overlook the serious sinfulness that chokes the life out of my soul. And yet God seems to have a fondness for thirsty women like me; he seems to gaze directly into my eyes and say to me, "A time has now come for you, a time to worship the Father in spirit and in truth."

At moments like those I know I will squirm, but I don't have to run away. I don't have to try to avoid the subject, to try to divert God's attention elsewhere. I think, for me at least, and maybe for you, it's time to stop trying to avoid his gaze and instead look squarely back into his eyes.

Time to recognize the unearthly compassion that he feels toward me.

Time to face up to the truth of my disappointing lifestyle and turn to him for help.

Time to finally say, "Yes, Lord. I'm listening."

Time to drink deeply from his well of loving, living water.

revealing the hope

The woman said, "I know that Messiah" (called Christ) "is coming. When he comes, he will explain everything to us."
Then Jesus declared, "I who speak to you am he."

—JOHN 4:25-26

She gasped for air without realizing it, eyes wide open and heart still racing.

Finally she noticed that the prophet had stopped talking, and she felt the pressure of knowing that it was now her turn to continue the conversation.

What could she say when face-to-face with eternal matters? What could she contribute to a conversation like that? She knew so little, really, despite her furtive pursuit of holy things amidst a life of unholy actions. Just enough to hope, to wish for something she assumed would probably never happen in her lifetime.

"I know Messiah is coming," she said at last, filling the silence with the one real truth that she knew and understood. "When he *comes, he will explain everything to us."*

For some reason she felt a sense of surrender — and comfort — in her own words. The Messiah was coming, even for Samaritans. Moses had promised it eons ago; it was a fact yet unrealized. He would come. She just hoped that when he did, she would be near enough to hear him speak words of truth. Words like the ones this prophet spoke to her today, at this well outside her hometown of Sychar.

There was an arrest of time, then, and something tickled at her soul, almost insisting that her spirit finally recognize what she already knew. She looked at the stranger, the Jew, the rabbi, the prophet before her, and her eyes grew wide at the bright flash of insight that erupted within her mind.

"I who speak to you," the prophet declared, "am he."

And again, she had trouble breathing.

I want to tell you a secret. It's at this point of John's narration that I begin to get really excited, that I start to realize this story will have a happy ending. Why? Because finally, at this single moment, the Woman at the Well begins to open up to the hope that stands before her.

"I know that Messiah is coming," she says.

It's a statement of surrender.

Until now she has challenged this Jewish stranger on every front. "You are a Jew and I am a Samaritan woman. How can you ask me for a drink?" (John 4:9). "Sir, you have nothing to draw with. . . . Where can you get this living water?" (John 4:11). "Are you greater than our father Jacob?" (John 4:12). "You Jews claim that the place where we must worship is in Jerusalem" (John 4:20).

Now, however, questions of water and requests for a drink and defense mechanisms and cultural accusations have all fallen helplessly aside. She breathes, she thinks, she longs for something she still can't see, something that Ambrose Bierce called "desire and expectation rolled into one"[1] and C. S. Lewis said was "a continual looking forward to the eternal world."[2] But she knows enough to know that she doesn't know enough.

"I know that Messiah is coming," she says. "When he comes, he will explain everything to us."

It is almost an empty hope. After all, they've been waiting for a messiah since the days of Moses. But like a little girl clinging to her daddy's promise, she stubbornly refuses to give up that hope. It's that yearning for the Christ that aches like a parched desert in her heart.

I can almost hear her thinking at this moment. *Okay, you win*, she must be saying to Jesus from inside her head. *I can't match up against the knowledge that you bring to this meeting, so I'm done trying. But I know that someday, someone is coming. Someone who will help me, who will fill my thirst for knowledge and show me all I need to know. Let's just leave it at that, okay?*

"I know that Messiah is coming."

It's an admission of need. A cry of surrender. A longing for hope.

And then Jesus reveals clearly, in no uncertain terms, exactly what she is both most afraid of and most thirsty for.

"I who speak to you," he says, "am he."

If Scripture is accurate in telling this story, Jesus' revelation of his true identity rendered this woman speechless. The hope of the world, the hope of her pitiful, wasted life was, at that moment, within hands' reach.

What was she going to do now?

Hope Calls to the Heart

One of my favorite Christian artists is Christine Dente of the husband-and-wife music group Out of the Grey. Recently I came upon one of my old favorites, their album *6.1*, and so I popped the CD into my truck and listened to it on the way to work. While driving, I was thinking about this particular time in the story of the Woman at the Well, wondering what this woman might have been thinking and feeling at the exact moment when Jesus declared his deity, "I who speak to you am he."

Just then the track changed on my CD player, and Christine Dente's song "With All My Heart" began to play. I was immediately mesmerized, barely breathing as I drove through traffic and listened to this song. Now, of course, I've had this album for years. I've heard this song a hundred times at the minimum. But something in that moment captured me, and I listened as if hearing it for the first time.

It's a hauntingly beautiful melody, with a tender, acoustic piano line that lingers in the ear and quivers out of the speakers like a butterfly carefully exploring a new garden. Really there's not much more to the song than that gentle piano fingering and Christine Dente's vocal delivery. Still, when I heard these lyrics flutter into my soul, the picture of the Woman at the Well in the moment of revelation was transfixed in my mind. I could almost see her standing, dusty-eyed, darkened skin, mouth partly open in wonder. Hope, real hope that fulfilled more than she could imagine, stood before her. She had to wonder — I still wonder at times — can this hope be trusted? Can this longing actually be satisfied? *Is this really the Christ?*

Listen to how Christine Dente describes that incommunicable moment:

> Hope calls to the heart of me, holding out his arms to
>   me
> I know he is mine but I must believe, with all my
>   heart . . .[3]

It is a striking image that Christine Dente offers, that of hope personified and holding out his arms toward us, and it's one that hearkens back to the days of ancient Rome.

During the heyday of the Roman Empire, its citizens were both the most civilized and among the most casually brutal people in all the world. Had you been a visitor to Rome at this time, you would have known that you'd arrived at the city limits (the *pomerium*) when you came upon a row of carefully placed white stones (called *cippi*) used to mark where the city began and the countryside ended. But before you crossed the *pomerium* into Rome, you would also be greeted by the smells of death and suffering and by the sounds of babies crying among the filth and heat.

You see, in this society, any unwanted infant was easily, and literally, disposed of. When a child was born with a deformity or under inauspicious circumstances or (as was too often the case) was simply a girl, if the parents didn't want the baby they would carry it to the city limits and toss it out with the garbage just outside the *cippi*. Here the human life that had just begun became a *res vacante* — something that its owner had abandoned.

Most of the babies out here would die from exposure or hunger or thirst. Some of the surviving ones would be taken as pets or slaves. A number of the girls would be collected and raised as prostitutes in various brothels. And, if the Roman fairy tales are to be believed, a precious few from the many would be rescued and adopted into families that wanted them. But, of course, in ancient Rome fairy tales rarely came true.[4]

At this time in Rome a father was considered the legal sovereign over his family and household. In fact one historian has noted that "the power of a [Roman] father is such that if he wishes to whip, starve, exile, or even in extreme cases kill his children then the law is powerless to stop him."[5] And so it was the father who decided whether or not a child became a daughter or just another tragic story among the *res vacante*.

After the agony of labor and childbirth, a mother would have to relinquish the fresh new life she'd brought into the world. The baby would then be laid at its father's feet, literally balancing there between life and death. If the father reached down and lifted the infant into his arms, the child would live, granted a home and a place as a member of that father's family. If the father ignored the baby and turned away from its firstborn breaths, the infant would be taken away, to the other side of the *pomerium*, where it would be abandoned and left to die.[6]

"I know that Messiah is coming."

When the Woman at the Well articulated that promise to

Jesus, she became like a Roman mother, relinquishing her hope to Christ and placing it, like a hungry, squalling infant, at his feet. I do not dare to presume to know the thoughts of Christ, but I suspect that he, in his compassion and insight, saw this woman's "desire and expectation rolled into one," that he recognized her "looking forward to the eternal world," and that he decided it was time to make known her hope's reality.

"I who speak to you am he," he said, and by doing that he figuratively assumed the role of the Roman father, reaching down and lifting up the helpless hope that the woman had lain before him, cradling that hope in his loving arms, saying in effect, "Yes, this hope will live. Yes, this hope belongs with me, in my household, just as you belong here as well."

Holding On to Hope

I think it's interesting that this woman would even *have* a hope of the Messiah still flickering within the dryness of her soul. Remember, she'd long ago abandoned the moral standards of her professed religious devotion. Yet if we are honest, we must admit, like this woman did, that the thirst we feel for intimacy with God never fully goes away, despite every foolish thing we do to drive God out of our lives. This hope of eternity acts upon our hearts and souls with a tenacity and fortitude that simply will not let us die in our own circumstances. For me, and for Christela Belle, this kind of determined persistence of hope is embodied in a heroic young man named Toussaint.

On July 8, 2007, Toussaint was just an average teenager attending school in his native country of Haiti. One of the other students at his school in Jacmel was a fifteen-year-old girl who was obviously pregnant, although she repeatedly denied it. On this fateful day Toussaint noticed this girl rushing away from the schoolhouse, with a noticeably smaller stomach and blood spattered on her legs. Moments later he followed her trail of blood and found himself in front of a row of outhouses used by the school. These crude toilets had been embedded in concrete and stood over deep pits in the ground where human waste seeped into the earth.

The bloodied girl was nowhere to be seen.

And then Toussaint heard a noise that made his heart skip a beat.

From deep inside a filthy, twenty-eight-foot toilet pit came the sounds of a baby gasping for air, choking and crying underneath the concrete.

Toussaint's classmate had given birth to a child and then thrown her baby girl down an outhouse toilet and left her for dead. The mother had given up hope, and as a result she was actively trying to kill her child and run away, literally, from both the responsibilities of motherhood and the infant she'd just brought into the world. But Toussaint would not let the hope of life die within him, and he refused to give up on the new person who had just been cruelly abandoned among the refuse.

Acting quickly, Toussaint first retrieved a rope and tried to lasso the infant from above the smelly septic pit. But the hole was too deep, and the concrete too immovable, and the young man couldn't reach the child that sputtered below him. Next he raced back to the school and called the police for help. Then he returned to the outhouse, determined to rescue that child at any cost.

Toussaint's phone call reached Darry "DJ" Williams, a US soldier working with a United Nations contingent in Haiti. When DJ and the Haitian police arrived on the scene, they found this heroic teen desperately chipping away at the concrete toilet, using makeshift tools to try to widen the opening so that he could go down and get the newborn out of that pit. After surveying the scene, DJ later reported, "I could see that the baby was moving and knew that time was of the essence." So he immediately called for more help, notifying the Sri Lankan army, also serving with the UN contingent, and asked for its assistance. The Sri Lankans arrived shortly and developed a plan.

Moving two stalls down, the soldiers quickly broke through the concrete foundation there, making a hole large enough for a man to fit through. Then they lowered a soldier down into the pit until he could reach the child. Carefully he wrapped the infant in a clean towel and secured the towel to a rope. Moments later the newborn was safely lifted out of the sewage, with umbilical cord and placenta still attached and intact.

After her ordeal the infant was raced to a hospital and then to an American orphanage equipped for medical care, the Hands and Feet Project in Haiti. DJ later marveled to the press about this miracle baby and said, "After being dropped thirty feet into a pit and left for dead, there were no bruises, no signs of trauma, and she was resting. I knew I had witnessed a miracle. Everyone involved knew it."

Today this once-lost infant is healthy and in the custody of people who love and care for her. When a policeman handed over the child to Hands and Feet Project, he said, "Christ must have been there for her." And so the baby was christened Christela, which means "Christ was there" in Haitian Creole. Her last name has been chosen as well, and it is Belle — which translates as "beautiful" in Creole. And so Christela Belle's new life begins. When she is old enough, she'll be told the story of her first few moments and the heroism of a teenage boy, Toussaint, who refused to give up hope of her rescue, who did everything in his power, who ably enlisted the aid of three different nations, just to save a newborn baby girl.[7]

I wonder if Toussaint was ever tempted to give in to despair over the plight of little Christela? After all, she was so far out of his reach, in the literal muck and mire of humanity. And he was just a teenage kid, still a child himself. Why should he bear the responsibility of another person's life? I guess because hope, once held, is so difficult to pry away. And hope, once realized, is worth all the hardship and heartache that comes from holding fast to its promise of something better.

As I said before, I see a picture of eternity in the tenacity and dogged persistence of Toussaint's effort to rescue Christela Belle, and I see a glimpse of that persistence in the way the Woman at the Well held on to the hope of a coming Messiah who would "explain everything" to her. Realistically, should she have clung to that hope with such desperate insistence? Probably not. She was hoping for a heavenly reward in spite of her lifestyle that denied heaven's precepts. But her circumstances were not enough to quench that hope, and Christ was so much greater than the sewage of her sins.

Jesus Christ Is the True Hope of the Heart

And that brings me to the most important part of this chapter, to the foundational truth that underscores both this page and all the other pages in this entire book:

Jesus Christ alone is the only true hope of the heart.

Gien Karssen knew something of this truth. As a young bride she and her husband lived in Europe during the 1940s. Only six weeks into their marriage, Hitler's police force arrested her husband, and he eventually perished in the Nazi Holocaust. But Gien's life did not end with the senseless death of her husband. After the war she traveled throughout Europe as a Christian minister, reaching out to women of all ages and sharing with them the hope found in a relationship with Christ.[8]

Some decades after World War II, Gien spent a little time exploring this moment when Jesus first revealed himself to be the hope of the Woman at the Well's heart. "A longing for the Messiah filled her heart," Gien wrote in her now-classic book, *Her Name Is Woman*:

> The Christ — he would clarify everything that was still dark and obscure. Right then the conversation reached its climax. Jesus assured her that her longing was fulfilled, the future could become present, then and there.
>
> "I am the Messiah." Christ was not a figure in a distant future. He was flesh and blood. He stood before her. What he had told no one else so plainly, he disclosed to her, "I am the Christ."

For her, only for her, he had come to the much-hated Samaria. For her he had bypassed the Jewish rules and regulations. The messianic hour had come. Time for discrimination was past. There was a solution for racial hatred and religious controversy. Every human being, even the most sinful, could now come to God through him.[9]

Gien's words strike me because they remind me of what I so often forget — and what I think the Woman at the Well spent nearly a lifetime forgetting. There is no hope, there is no human desire or lauded expectation that will ever fulfill the promise of a relationship with God. We seek satisfaction in so many different ways; we long for the approval of our parents and our peers; we do just about anything we think will make us just a little bit happier. We chase after religion, education, youth, beauty, money, and more. Yet even when we attain these temporary things, psychological studies reveal that we still find our inmost hopes living unfulfilled.[10] Why? Because we attach hope — hope that should rest only in God — onto other people or situations who, out of basic definition, will always fail us.

Still, we can't feel too judgmental toward ourselves in this regard. If the Woman at the Well is any indication, we've been doing this kind of bait and switch with hope for centuries of human history. She longed for the Messiah, yet she settled for a series of unfulfilling relationships and halfhearted theological arguments instead. And you and I, dear friend, can't continue to let ourselves be taken in by this kind of guaranteed disappointment either. If we know that Christ alone offers the only secure hope, we must learn to seek him first and foremost, to place our hopes and dreams squarely in his hands. No person, no circumstance, no wealth or prestige or anything else in this life can ever be a substitute for the hope inherent in intimacy with God. This is a lesson that breaks my heart, because we've all seen too many of our sisters experience the heartache and pain of misplaced hope.

Just recently I was walking on a treadmill at the gym, doing my part to keep this body of mine healthy. (Hey, I am getting older after all!) At my gym they have a "theater room" where they show films on a big-screen TV; you can exercise and also plug in your headphones to enjoy a movie during your workout. So there I was, watching a portion of the Academy Award–winning film *Million Dollar Baby*. This movie stars Hilary Swank as Maggie, a hard-working, aspiring female boxer. Her gruff and grizzled trainer is Frankie Dunn (played by Clint Eastwood), and her welfare-guzzling "trailer trash" mother is Earline (played to perfection by Margo Martindale).

Maggie has worked her way out of poverty and is finally beginning to see some financial gains as a result of her successes in the ring. Still, she barely spends any of her money, socking away one fight purse after another, and continuing to live a meager lifestyle. Finally the reason comes out. Maggie has one real hope in life: to make her mama proud. So she has scrimped and saved and sacrificed until she finally has enough money to make a grand gesture of love and dedication to her mother.

On the day she plans to make this grand gesture, Maggie arrives with Frankie at her mother's rusted-out home in a downtrodden trailer park. With grinning anticipation Maggie picks up Earline and drives her to the big surprise. They pull into the driveway of an empty house, clean, fresh, and ready to move into. With a smile wider than sunshine, Maggie opens the front door and ushers her mother in. "It's all yours, Mama!" she says.

"You bought this for me?" Earline says.

"Yep, all yours, free and clear!" Maggie is practically bursting with pleasure at this moment.

"You shouldn't have done this," Earline says.

"You need a decent place," Maggie says kindly, admiring the home, and unaware that her mother is getting angry.

"You shouldn't have done it!" Earline shouts at her suddenly. "You should have asked me first! Darlin', the government's gonna find out about this house and they're gonna stop my welfare . . . I can't live without my welfare."

Maggie's face is turned away from the camera now, but we can hear the pain etched in it through the sound of her voice. It's obvious she is no longer smiling.

"Mama, I send you money," she says quietly.

"What about my medicine?" Earline continues to rant. "Medicaid gonna cut me off! How am I supposed to get my medicine?"

Now we see Maggie's face in a close-up. It's still battered and bruised from her last boxing match, but the real pain is in her eyes. "I'll send you more money," she says earnestly. But she might as well be saying, "Mama, please. Love me. Accept me. Tell me you're proud of me. It's the only thing I've hoped for as long as I can remember." Those are the words whispered in her downcast eyes.

"Why didn't you just give me the money?" Earline snorts with loathing. "Why'd you have to buy me a house?" She shakes her head in utter disappointment at her daughter.

Back at the trailer park mother and daughter deliver awkward good-byes, and only now does Earline notice her daughter's facial cuts and swollen eyes.

"It's from the fight," a subdued Maggie says. "I'm a fighter, Mama."

"Find a man," Earline says with disgust. "Live proper. People hear about what you're doing and they laugh . . . they laugh at you."[11]

I'm not ashamed to tell you that when this scene from *Million Dollar Baby* began to unspool in front of me at the gym, I simply couldn't take it. Having seen the movie before, I knew what was about to happen, and it made me feel a sadness deep in the pit of my stomach. So much so that I actually cut short my workout, unplugged my headphones, and walked out of the gym. I simply couldn't bear to watch Maggie's hopes — for a mother's love, for acceptance, for approval — be so callously and casually crushed under the hurtful words and attitudes of her ungrateful mama.

And you know what? I can't bear to sit by and watch you go through the same kind of disappointment either, because if you miss the hope of Christ, you'll go through Maggie's kind of disappointment over and over. Again and again.

We must learn, you and I, to bypass the easy hopes of temporary circumstances and instead embrace what I call the difficult hope of complete dependence on Christ alone for every emotional, spiritual, and physical need. To accept that Christ alone is the true hope of the heart for thirsty women like Maggie, like me, and like you. To say to ourselves, as the Woman at the Well once did, "I know that the Messiah is coming into my situation, into my heartache, into my desperate need, into my family relationships, into my career problems, into my legal problems, into my financial circumstances, into every moment of my life. And when he comes, he will explain everything to me."

When that happens, it doesn't mean that all our problems will magically vanish or that all the mistakes of our past will suddenly be rendered irrelevant. But it does mean that if we can determine to place our trust in this difficult hope of intimate moments with Jesus, we can find eternal purpose in our temporary longings and heavenly peace in any earthly circumstance.

Wanda Luttrell is a mother who knows something of this difficult hope. As the parent of one she calls a "prodigal," she has spent decades dealing with a son who can't seem to find his way in the world. Her heart cries out daily over her boy who's gone astray. "When I stand listening to my adult child's angry tirades at me, at God, at life in general, do I hate him?" she says. "No, I just want to take him in my arms and soothe his troubled soul back to peace in God, as I once soothed his troubled dreams back to peaceful sleep. I want to help him find his way out of darkness and confusion into a fulfilling life."[12]

In this situation Wanda has learned something of the difficult hope, of turning to Christ as her heart's one true aspiration for her son. And along the way she has also gleaned a little insight into the heart of God. These are things that I believe the Woman at the Well also learned when Jesus interrupted her life with the statement that *he* was the hope she had longed for, that he who spoke to her was indeed the Christ. I think Wanda's words are so eloquent on this subject that I want to ask her to end this chapter for me.

Drink deeply of Wanda's wisdom, sister — about hope, about Christ, and about the heart of God for you and me. I know I did:

A mother gets no joy from seeing her child reap what he has sown. She suffers along with him, holds out her arms, and says, "Come, and I will help you pick up the pieces."

Isn't that just like God? We may refer to him as "our Father" and describe him in masculine terms, but God surely has a mother's heart. He accepts the fact that we have messed up his best intentions for our lives and holds out his hand. "Come, let's see what you and I can make of what's left." And he can take the most shattered individual, the one who not only missed God's plan A, B, and C for his life, but even X, Y, and Z, and put it all back together into something beautiful.

He *can* do this because he is God. He *will* do this because he loves us. Enough to die for us.[13]

processing the revelation

Just then his disciples returned and were surprised to find him talking with a woman. But no one asked, "What do you want?" or "Why are you talking with her?"

Then, leaving her water jar, the woman went back to the town.

—John 4:27-28

They stood in silence then, he comfortable and at peace, she as still as a pond on the outside and raging like a white-water river inside.

Had he just said what she thought he said? Did he just look her straight in the eyes and declare himself to be the actual Messiah, the Christ of God?

And could it be true?

At first she felt that she must say something in response, as though it was expected for her to say, "Of course you are," and immediately fall at his feet or something. But in truth she felt more like saying, "Of course you are . . . crazy!" and running headlong in the opposite direction. But that impulse soon quelled itself in the quiet sanity of the moment. Well, not the running part, but at least the crazy part.

She looked at him in wonder. Could it be?

He looked back at her with compassion and patience, and as he did when she first saw him at the well, he waited. He said nothing more. He made no attempts to convince her of his truth, to lay out the facts behind his ludicrous (or was it really?) claim to deity. He didn't even ask what she thought of his latest revelation.

Moments ago this man was simply a stranger to her, invading her daily routine. Then he was just another lazy Jew, a domineering and despised man ready to take advantage of her kindness in dipping at the well. And a hypocrite breaking his own religious rules to boot. Then he was more than a hypocrite, instead a rabbi and teacher — but still less than a friend, and still a hated Jew. Suddenly he'd shown himself to be even more than that. He was, by all evidence, a prophet of some sort, a holy man. And now, at last, he was the entire opposite of everything she'd first thought him to be.

He claimed to be the Messiah. Her Messiah.

It was ridiculous that he would make that claim. Yet even more absurd was that she was tempted to believe it. That she, a skeptical, distrusting, sinful, solitary Samaritan woman would be visited — in person — by the Messiah was the stuff of fairy tales.

And oh, how she hoped it was true.

But she had been deceived before, and it could happen again, right here, today. She inhaled deeply and realized that she, too, had become comfortable with the silence between them. There was an unspoken trust. He was not going to harm her, nor *pressure her. She was going to take the time she needed to consider his words — and his claim.*

All too soon that moment of silent trust was broken, though. Almost as if from nowhere, several men appeared at the well. They were carrying food and supplies, and from the way the would-be Messiah greeted them, it was apparent they were his followers.

Of course he'd have followers. What kind of Messiah would wander the world alone?

Immediately the peace of the place was shattered. They didn't say anything against her — didn't say much at all beyond their greetings, actually — but she could read their looks. She was reminded again of two things: She was a Samaritan woman, and Jews hated Samaritans. The frowns and grumbling coughs communicated that much.

Still, no one said a curse or even questioned the Master about his discourse with her, and that was something she wouldn't have expected. She let her eyes scan the new arrivals, trying to quickly judge which ones would be her antagonists, and which ones would sit idly by, watching the others pass judgment.

Then a motion caught the corner of her eye. She turned her head and saw the stranger (the Messiah?) stroll a few feet over until he stood between her and the other men. No one said a word, but it was obvious he was placing his protection upon her. She was not to be bothered by racial and religious bigotry.

She had more important things to worry about.

She felt her feet slowly backing away from the well, then she turned toward the city and picked up speed. No matter though, because even by the time she was fairly running back to Sychar, her brain was still working faster than her legs.

Could this be . . .? she wondered the whole way back to town.

Only when she reentered the city limits did she notice that she'd left her water jar at the well. But it didn't matter.

She had more important things to worry about.

Ever sit through a moment of truly awkward silence? You know, the kind where everybody desperately wants to move the conversation along, perhaps to relieve the tension of a strained relationship, perhaps to alleviate the pressure of a social situation or maybe to cover up after an insulting conversational error. In these kinds of situations every second seems to tick off in slow motion, and minutes can seem like hours. The mind races at top speed, searching for the right words to say, the right way to defuse the anxiety filling the room with every passing breath.

Should you make a joke? Confront the issue head on? Ignore it completely? Politely excuse yourself? Do nothing? Or do something else completely?

It was a moment like this that punctuated the meeting between Christ and the Woman at the Well. Just when things got really interesting — just when Jesus declared his own deity — the disciples returned to the well and silenced the conversation completely.

Remember Christ's disciples? Way back at the beginning of this story we were told that they had gone into the town to buy food. Now they've returned with bread and other food, ready to share their recently acquired bounty with their leader and rabbi. But as soon as they arrive, the food is forgotten, the idle chatter these disciples must have shared between themselves while walking is choked off, and—awkwardly—everyone stands around the well in silence.

There is Jesus. They'd left him alone. Now he was not.

There is the Woman at the Well. A Samaritan. Someone whom no good Jew, especially a good Jewish man, would even deign to speak to.

There are the disciples, taking in the scene, doubts and accusations racing through their minds. Still, no one is ready to question what Jesus is doing at this point.

And hanging in the air between them all, like dirty laundry slung over a line, is Jesus' assertion that he, in fact, is the promised Messiah of God.

I think the disciples must have been frowning when they came to the well.

I expect that the woman probably wore a look of surprise that quickly turned to concern when she saw the other Jewish men amble up to her well.

And Jesus? Believe it or not, I like to think that he might have been grinning.

God Doesn't Run from Silence

Let me explain what I mean.

Something about silence inherently makes most people uncomfortable. Remember a time when you were on a first date and there was uncomfortable silence? Or sitting near someone at the hospital and not knowing what to say? That feeling of wishing someone would say something, *anything*, to move the conversation along? It was that crashing quiet that descended onto this scene that obviously unnerved both Jesus' disciples and the Woman at the Well. Their immediate reactions seem to indicate that is true.

Consider first the disciples. Upon returning from their errand, they found that their religious authority figure, the one in whom they had placed their trust for spiritual truth, the one for whom they had left all their earthly possessions, was now blatantly and deliberately breaking the religious morality of that day.

As theologian Craig Keener reminds us,

Jewish piety warned men not to talk much with women . . . both because of temptation and because of what others might think. That the disciples are amazed yet trust their teacher enough not to ask about the situation is a sign of their respect for him.

The apostle John — who was one of the disciples present at this moment — reports that they were all "surprised to find him [Jesus] talking to a woman." But the simple fact that it was *Christ* who was doing the talking was enough to prevent them from hurling accusations at the woman or snarling, "What do *you* want?" in her direction. And their deep respect for Jesus kept them from asking him, "Why are you talking with *her*?"

Left with no other options, they are all speechless. The result, from their perspective, was an uncomfortable silence over the apparently immoral behavior of Christ.

The Woman at the Well stood on the other side of this equation. And she knew that it was considered a sin for her to "tempt"

Jesus by talking to him so brazenly, as a woman acting equal to a man. She must have felt a twinge of fear at the sight of the disciples. Would they hurt her? Accuse her of breaking the law? Insult and abuse her? And what about Jesus . . . had he really just claimed to be the Messiah? Was he the Messiah or just a pretender to glory? If he were the Messiah, what would he do to a sinful woman like her? Or tell his disciples to do to her?

Left with all these questions and uncertainties in her mind, she was speechless. The result, from her perspective, was an uncomfortable silence over what the next reaction of all these hateful Jewish men might be toward her.

In the middle of it all was Jesus himself, the serene instigator of all the discomfort and the one whose words and actions have silenced everyone around him. But for some reason, I don't see him as fidgeting nervously beside the well. I don't think he was uncomfortable in the slightest, either by the people or by the silence. I believe he knew what was happening inside the minds and hearts of his disciples and the Woman at the Well. I believe he looked into that singular moment and saw the story unfolding to its completion through the end of time. I think he must have been prepared for the silence that fell on the scene, in that dusty place, outside the town of Sychar in Samaria.

I think that Jesus, unlike the others, must have been the only person at peace with that moment, and thus was completely comfortable with the silence that surrounded him And, because I believe Christ must have a compassionate sense of humor, I think he probably looked at all the tension and worry in the faces of those around him — and that he might have grinned at the others as if to say, "Hey, don't sweat it. I know what I'm doing."

To put it another way: *God doesn't run away from silence.*

Sure, when we are in those moments of relational discomfort, our natural reaction is to fill the quiet spots with idle chatter or angry words. We run from the silence between us by speaking words or throwing nervous laughter over it, trying to mask the discomfort that it makes us feel.

God, on the other hand, seems to be quite comfortable when nothing is said. In fact he seems to prefer it at times (see Psalm 46:10; Proverbs 17:1; Mark 6:31-32, among other Scriptures in the Bible). Nowhere in Scripture is God made to feel ill at ease when quiet arises between people.

Mother Teresa summed it up beautifully when she once said, "God is the friend of silence. See how nature — trees, flowers, grass — grows in silence. See the stars, the moon, and the sun how they move in silence . . . we need silence to be able to touch souls."[2]

And I believe that's what was happening at this particular instant in Christ's meeting the Woman at the Well. In these hushed moments the Holy Spirit was speaking most plainly to her, echoing into her heart the revelation that Jesus had just delivered to her. It should come as no surprise that she needed a few minutes to process that divine declaration!

The light of God's love was in its first glow within this woman's intellect. The first drops of living rain were finally beginning to penetrate her thirsty, parched soul. She needed a moment, maybe two, to let that water soak beneath the surface of her understanding, to let that glow warm and freshen her very being. The silence was necessary, because in that silence the Holy Spirit was asking her the question that she would later ask her neighbors, "Could this be the Christ?"

When I get to heaven, it won't surprise me at all if I find out that Jesus himself orchestrated the moment when the disciples returned in such a way as to guarantee that they would be shocked speechless. It would be well within his character to have put into place that kind of protective circumstance to allow this thirsty woman a few precious moments of silence to begin to process the revelation that he was indeed her promised Messiah.

Still, that kind of silence can be a little frightening for us human folk. It apparently was for the Woman at the Well. In that awkward stillness of revelation and accusation, she let her instincts take over.

And she ran away.

Sometimes God Lets the Runaway Run Away

The scriptural history describes it this way: "Leaving her water jar, the woman went back to the town."

Forgotten was her original intent of gathering water for her daily use. Gone was her foolish bravado and attempts at verbal sparring with this Jewish stranger. In the most basic human reaction, it was time for "fight or flight" — and she chose flight!

When I read this moment in the historical record, I have to admit that the background music I hear in my head is "Brave, brave, Sir Robin — he bravely ran away!" (Pardon my Monty Python reference there.)

The interesting thing here is that Jesus didn't chase after this runaway; he didn't send his disciples to bring her back so he could explain more or clarify what he had meant or even answer the questions that were obviously running through her head. He sat there and did nothing. He let her run away.

During my college years I worked for a while as a salesperson for a national chain of jewelry stores. One bit of advice I heard regularly from my bosses was the importance of closing the sale and asking the customers to buy whatever it was I had been showing them. Every time a customer looked at a ring or necklace or bracelet or whatever — no matter how long or how short the amount of time spent examining it was — my responsibility was the same. Before I put that article of jewelry back in the case, it was my job to ask the customer if he or she wanted to buy it.

Many times I thought a customer was absolutely *not* interested in something I'd just shown her, but I would ask anyway: "Would you like me to ring this up for you?" You'd be surprised (along with me!) at how many times that apparently noncommittal customer would respond with, "Sure, I'll take it." And I always wondered what would have happened if I hadn't asked.

I tell you about that experience because it seems as though Jesus was a rotten salesperson! Here he had a captive audience in the Woman at the Well, someone who was obviously interested in what he was offering. Yet when it came time to close the sale, to ask for a commitment of faith from his target customer, he simply let her walk away without saying a word and without moving a muscle to try to stop her.

However (and this is the important part), Jesus wasn't trying to *sell* anything to anyone, least of all to this thirsty woman who came alone to Jacob's well by the town of Sychar. His purpose was not another notch in his ledger of souls, nor another victory in an evangelistic crusade.

So he let the runaway run away.

He gave her the time and space to begin processing the revelation of his identity. The hurried, harried person within me squirms at that kind of patience and serenity on display in the personality of Christ. But he began this little encounter by waiting for the woman to come to the well, so it should come as no surprise to me that he was willing to wait a little longer for her to come back to find faith in him as well.

Some theologians presume that our thirsty heroine left simply because she had immediately believed Jesus' declaration and thus ran off to obediently "be a witness" who told others about Christ.[3] But I think Lawrence Richards explains it best when he says, "For the Samaritan woman faith came hard because she knew she was a great sinner. Her sense of worth was worn away. How hard it was for her to realize that God valued her and wanted her to become a worshiper. How hard to believe that he was offering her eternal life as her love gift."[4]

In short I believe that at that moment the Woman at the Well just wanted to — had to — get away, to clear her head, and to sort through the implications of Jesus' last statement. Was he the Christ? Could he be believed? Could he be trusted? She didn't know, but she was determined to find out. So she ran away to think it over, to puzzle it through, to replay their conversation in her head, and maybe to talk it over with others she knew back in the town of Sychar.

And Christ was willing to give her the time she needed, so he let her run back to town. It was as if he knew something special that she did not know . . . which, of course, he did.

You Can Run from God, but You Can't Run Away from God

In 2006, Terry Esau decided to conduct a unique experiment in his relationship with Jesus. Instead of praying his normal list of daily requests, he would pray only three words: "Surprise me, God." And he would pray that way for thirty days straight, journaling his experience during those days.

In the middle of that time, Terry had this little revelation:

> I've noticed something interesting about this Surprise
> Me experiment: virtually all of my "surprises" so far fall
> into one of two categories — people and God . . . I seem
> to run into that God guy almost everywhere, or maybe
> he runs into me (with one of us invisible, it's difficult to
> tell who ran into whom).

Terry, it seems, discovered what the Woman at the Well first realized several thousand years ago:

You can run from God, but you can't run *away* from God.

When she left Christ at the well, the woman probably thought she was going to be safe from his unnerving questions and uncomfortable spiritual insight. But with each step she took, the words he spoke seemed to weigh more deeply on her mind, consuming her thoughts and flooding her soul with both excitement and confusion. She ran away physically from God, but her heart could never truly evade his presence, her mind couldn't shake the truth of his word, her soul couldn't run away from the living water that poured from his spirit into hers.

You cannot escape God; you can only pretend to hide from him, like a child who is unaware of the true nature of his world. I remember when my son was a toddler he would occasionally play hide-and-seek with me by covering his own eyes with his hands. In his precious little mind he thought that if he could not see me, then I could not see him. His joy at being "found" behind his hands made playing this silly game with him worth gold to me!

Sometimes, though, we try to play that silly game ourselves — with God. We assume that if we're not speaking to him, then that means he's not speaking to us. We run from his Word, the Bible. We run from his church. We run from prayer and intimacy with Jesus. But through it all, God waits patiently, seeing the truth, speaking to us in ways that we don't recognize or understand. And wherever we go, he is there, active in our hearts and minds and souls and lives, whether we know it or not.

Let me put that in more, um, theological terms:

God is like a bunny. (Stick with me on this!)

Oh, not just *any* bunny. One particular bunny. One very special bunny. A bunny first created by Margaret Wise Brown in a classic children's book. Here's how the story goes:

In *The Runaway Bunny* the mother of a brash little rabbit hears her child announce one day, "I am running away."

The mother is unfazed. She says simply, "If you run away, I will run after you. For you are my little bunny."

The would-be runaway isn't so easily stymied, however. He announces that if she runs after him, he will turn into a fish and swim away in a stream.

Says the mother, "If you become a fish in a trout stream, I will become a fisherman and I will fish for you."

And so it goes. The little bunny says he will become a rock on a mountain, a flower in a hidden garden, a bird, a sailboat, and more. And for each new obstacle, the mother bunny has a plan, promising to pursue her child as a mountain climber, a gardener, a tree for resting birds, the wind in a sailboat's sails, and so on.

Finally our little runaway realizes that nothing he can do will cause him to lose the relentless love of his mother. "Shucks," he finally says at the end of the story, "I might just as well stay where I am and be your little bunny."[6]

This kind of relentless "bunny love" is what that Woman at the Well experienced firsthand, and it's a perfect example of how Jesus' persistent love continues to chase after you and me.

No matter where we may try to run from Jesus' love, no matter what tactics we invent to shield ourselves from His embrace, no matter what circumstances in life threaten to separate us from him, God's love never wanes, never fades, never flickers or dims. His is a relentless, unwavering love that pursues us over hill and dale, under the shadows of sadness and in the sunshine of joy. Like that mother bunny, Jesus will always, *always* come after us. He proved that centuries ago when he refused to let a nameless woman beside an ancient well go thirsty for eternity, when he met her in the middle of the day and challenged her to face down the reality of her hidden sins, and when he let her run from his person — but refused to let her run away from his presence.

And that's when the good stuff really began.

examining the christ

And [she] said to the people, "Come, see a man who told me everything I ever did. Could this be the Christ?" They came out of the town and made their way toward him.

— JOHN 4:28-30

Almost out of habit, her feet carried her to the marketplace in the center of town. Lost in her thoughts as she was, she wasn't really aware of where she was going until she got there. At first she hesitated. These people generally were not her friends, more like reluctant acquaintances really. Still, the churning within her had to be dealt with, and while they might not like her here, they would listen to her — and maybe, just maybe, they would help her.

The words spilled out almost of their own accord, like a child telling of some wonderful sight up in a tree or a gossip sharing some really juicy new secrets to her closest friends.

"Come, see a man who told me everything I ever did!"

She fairly shouted it among the stalls of the marketplace, and heads that would normally have ignored her arrival suddenly *snapped toward her. A few men stepped her direction, curiosity written on their faces.*

"Come see!" she said again, trembling with excitement now. "He told me everything I ever did. Could this be the Christ?"

A few women sniffed her direction and turned away. But several men and other women and a handful of children came closer. The questions came fast. What was she talking about? Whom had she seen? Could who *be the Messiah?*

Could this be the Messiah? *She kept asking herself this question every time she posed it to the growing crowd.*

"Come see!" she pleaded. "Come see a man who told me everything I ever did! Could this be the Christ?"

Finally one man, then another, then several turned toward Jacob's well. In moments an entire crowd of Samaritans was marching out of the city to see the man she'd left by the well. For a moment she had a fear that perhaps he and his disciples had already given up on Sychar, that maybe he had already left their city and gone on to who-knows-where in the distant countryside. She quickly fell in step with the others, hurrying them toward the well outside of town. She needn't have worried, though, because when they all got back to the well, they found the man doing for the crowd what he'd done for her.

He was waiting.

"Could this be the Christ?"

That one question has echoed through the halls of history like a gong, demanding not just an answer but also careful consideration from anyone who hears it. When the Woman at the Well was confronted with the Messiah himself, when she had stared face-to-face with the one who was everything she had hoped and dreamed of, the first thing she did was run away. The second thing she did was seek a second opinion!

Racing back into Sychar, this woman apparently disrupted whatever was going on in the social center of the town. "Come see a man who told me everything I ever did," she said breath-lessly. "Could this be the Christ?"

I have to admit that I am a little bewildered and a little amused when I read the scholarly commentaries and high-minded theo-logical opinions that address this part of the story. Many seem to miss the basic, emotional response of a thirsty woman confronted for the first time with the literal man of her dreams. For instance, esteemed scholars John Walvoord and Roy Zuck read this portion of Scripture and ascribe unexpected evangelistic weightiness to this simple question of a thirsty woman. They say:

> Literally, her question was, "This couldn't be the
> Messiah, could it?" The question expected a tentative
> negative answer. She framed the question this way,
> in all probability, because she knew the people would
> not respond favorably to a dogmatic assertion from a
> woman, especially one of her reputation. Just as Jesus
> had captured her attention by curiosity, so she raised the
> people's curiosity.[1]

Now please understand that I hold Dr. Walvoord and Dr. Zuck in the highest regard. That said, however, I think these two wise men have completely missed a point that might seem obvious to a woman. They've interpreted this woman's actions through the backward lens of systematic theology, of church missiology, and of evangelistic intent. These intellectual men have made an assumption about this woman's motivation for action and have decided that her immediate response to Christ's announcement of his identity was also an intellectual one rather than an emotional one. Their conclusion assumes that she instantly formulated an elaborate rhetorical exercise designed to elicit a favorable response from a skeptical hometown audience and thus convert them to the Christianity she had only moments ago discovered. To me that seems a bit of a stretch.

You know what I think? I suspect this thirsty woman dropped her water jar, raced back to town and asked "Could this be the Christ?" for one reason only:

She wanted to know if this could be the Christ!

It doesn't take a theologian or a scholar to see that simple fact. Our precious heroine beside the well had finally been tempted by belief; for the first time in her life, the thirst she felt inside her soul was being enticed by rivers of living water flowing out from the stranger who claimed to be the Christ. So she did what anyone would do in that situation — she sought input from others she knew, and perhaps some she trusted. She invited her whole town to come out and scrutinize this would-be Messiah, to place him under the microscope and help her search out the answer to that all-important question: *Could this be the Christ?*

Perhaps the theologians I've read are simply blessed with a more ready faith than mine and thus are comfortably confident in their assumptions of instantaneous trust and evangelistic response in the real-life people of the biblical histories. My faith comes so much harder, so much more filled with doubt and uncertainty. And so perhaps my perception that this woman of old needed time and assurance before accepting Jesus as the Christ is as flawed as I perceive others' perceptions to be. But when I read about the Woman at the Well, I see a woman who is more like you and me than like an academic; I see a woman whose emotions run the gamut when embraced by Christ, whose mind struggles to understand the eternal truth being flooded into her being. I see a woman who is thirsty, just beginning to realize that living water can indeed quench the desires of her soul.

And I see a woman who, like me, has been burned a few times before. Someone who has been hurt and betrayed by others and untruth in the past. Someone who desperately *wants* to believe, but also cautiously approaches belief with a few reality-inspired questions. Someone who is not afraid to let a little doubt protect her from a lot of disillusionment. So it comes as no surprise to me that she would hurry back to town, that she would ask for help in tackling the most important question she'll ever consider: "Could this be the Christ?"

Faith Starts with a Question

As you have probably guessed by the many references I've made to him in this book, I am fascinated by the life and personality of the apostle Paul. Arguably the most influential theologian of all time, he wrote most of the New Testament — and also was Christianity's first-recorded true missionary in the modern sense of that word.

Have you ever read the account of when he, like the Woman at the Well, first came face-to-face with the Christ? His story is recorded in Acts 9:1-6:

> Meanwhile, Saul [Paul] was still breathing out murder-ous threats against the Lord's disciples. He went to the high priest and asked him for letters to the syna-gogues in Damascus, so that if he found any there who belonged to the Way, whether men or women, he might take them as prisoners to Jerusalem. As he neared Damascus on his journey, suddenly a light from heaven flashed around him. He fell to the ground and heard a voice say to him, "Saul, Saul, why do you persecute me?"
> *"Who are you, Lord?" Saul asked.* (italics mine)
> "I am Jesus, whom you are persecuting," he replied.

Do you see what Paul's immediate response was on that road to Damascus? When that blinding light bore down on him from heaven, his first response was to ask the nitty-gritty ques-tion: "Who are you, Lord?" The subsequent answer changed not only Paul's life but also the course of history for anyone who might later be influenced by Paul and his ministry — you and me included.

My husband, Mike, has never been accosted by Jesus on a road to anywhere — let alone on a road to Damascus — but his faith experience also began with a question or two.

"For me," Mike says, "there was a time in my teenage years when I decided I couldn't simply accept whatever my parents or other leaders taught me about faith. I had to find out for myself what was true and what wasn't. So I boiled everything down and asked myself this hard question: Is there a God? After a few weeks of going through the logic and evidence I could find on that subject, I finally reached a point where I could say, 'Yes, there is a God.' Then came the second, harder question: If there is a God, then who is it?"[2]

Mike, like the apostle Paul, basically asked a question that was a variant on the theme of the Woman at the Well's query to her hometown: Could Jesus be the Christ? Mike spent several more weeks exploring that question, asking more questions, studying religions like Hinduism, Islam, Eastern mysticism, and even ancient Greek and Roman mythologies. In the end Mike says:

> At one point during my exploration, I started noticing a pattern. Every major modern religion — Islam, Buddhism, Judaism — acknowledged that Jesus was a "good teacher" and an admirable religious leader, but they stopped short of acknowledging that he might be the Christ, the actual son of God. Yet Jesus himself claimed those things.[3] If he were not the Christ and the actual Son of God, then he did not deserve to be lauded as a "good teacher" or an admirable religious leader because he was lying or was terribly deceived about his own identity — and his deception had cost millions more than just their lives, but also their very souls.
>
> But if he was the Christ, then all those other religions giving grudging, halfhearted approval to him was simply not good enough. It was like saying "Hitler was a good man, except for that whole genocide of the Jews thing." That kind of thinking is absurd.

Either Jesus is who he claimed to be, and thus deserved nothing less than utter devotion, or he wasn't who he claimed to be and thus deserved utter contempt. There could be no middle ground.[4]

If you've read any of my husband's many books (and if you haven't, you should!), you know where he ended up. For Mike the single answer to all his questions was the same one that the apostle Paul discovered and the same one that the Woman at the Well also heard: Jesus is indeed the Christ.

What I wonder sometimes is this: What would have happened if Mike, or Paul, or the Woman at the Well had never asked those hard questions of faith about Jesus Christ? What if they'd never said, "Could this be the Christ?" or "Who are you, Lord?" Would they have reached that moment of rock-solid faith that could (ideally!) move mountains? Would they have dared to pursue that life-changing, soul-quenching intimacy with God himself? Or would they have continued seeking water and finding only dust in the tenets and half-truths of other philosophies and world religious propaganda?

For that matter, what would happen if Mike, or you, or I today, stopped asking the hard questions of faith about Christ? Because we publish a monthly Internet magazine for families, Mike and I often get e-mail from parents and other readers in response to our writing. I remember one time, several years ago, there was a national outcry among religious leaders over some new line of popular toys and cartoons. Several prominent Christian voices came out strongly against these toys and in favor of Christian boycotts and economic pressures on toymakers and so on. So Mike decided to investigate the phenomenon.

He played with the toys and games, watched the cartoons, read all the literature. Then he made a list of all the things that Christian leaders said were supposedly immoral about these toys and discovered that the arguments against this line of toys were ones that could be used against any toy or game — even the time-honored game of chess. So we published an article that pointed that out and suggested that maybe Christian parents were over-reacting in regard to these relatively innocuous toys.

The response was overwhelming — and sadly surprising. Many well-meaning Christian people took Mike to task for "daring to question our respected Christian leaders." For the dozens of readers who sent us reprimands, the greatest evil was not necessarily the toys but the fact that Mike would be so impudent as to *ask a question* about a real-life application of practical theology in a parent and a child's life.

Through that experience, and many like it, I've come to understand a few important things. First is that questions are not the enemy of God. Rather, questions are most often the beginning of the life of faith — and subsequently, sincere questions often become the lifeblood of an authentic relationship with Jesus.

The second thing I've learned is that questions and doubts never negate the truth. Rather, diligent scrutiny of an idea or assertion actually confirms the truth. If it did not, the supposed truth would be nothing more than mere speculation at best, or an outright lie at worst.

Questioning Truth Confirms the Truth

Many years ago, back in 1991, I read a story about an eight-year-old boy named Anthony Henderson. Young Anthony was a student at Barcroft Elementary School in Arlington, Virginia, and as luck would have it, that school had recently been named a "Point of Light" by then-president of the United States, George H. W. Bush. To celebrate this honor, President Bush made plans for a personal appearance at Anthony's school.

Anthony was going to meet the president!

All week long preparations were made, teachers instructed kids on how to behave for the president, told them what to expect to happen, and so on. Finally the fateful day arrived. A long, black limousine pulled up outside the school, and Anthony watched as several muscular bodyguards in dark suits ushered a tall man with glasses into the school.

Anthony took a closer look. They said this guy was President George H. W. Bush, but was it really? He seemed so tall . . . taller than what the president looked like on TV. Uncertainty filled the boy until he finally asked, "Are you really the president?"

The tall man sat down next to Anthony at a table, smiled, and said, "Yeah!" Then he reached for his wallet and said, "Let me see if I've got an ID." Pulling out his driver's license, he gave it to Anthony to investigate. Then he showed off some family pictures and even let Anthony examine his American Express card.

Yep, this guy was who he said he was: the president of the United States! For Anthony that meant he had a chance to have a conversation with the most powerful political leader in the world. He also got an autograph and some "inside information" about the president's family and interests. In short he got the memory of a lifetime—a personal meeting with the president.[5]

Listen, dear friend, Anthony Henderson's questioning of the elder Bush's identity certainly did not negate that man's office of the presidency. What it did was provide an opportunity for the truth of that presidency to be scrutinized and subsequently affirmed beyond any doubt.

Likewise, when the Woman at the Well raced back to town and shouted, "Could this be the Christ?" her doubts and questions in no way negated the truth of Jesus' real identity. What it did was provide an opportunity for Jesus' outrageous claims of deity to be scrutinized by everyone in Sychar—and to subsequently be affirmed by their own firsthand experience.

You see, unlike the elder George Bush, Jesus didn't claim to be simply some influential political leader. No, he claimed to be God incarnate. Creator of all. The promised Messiah. Son of God wrapped in flesh, come to redeem the world he made. And when someone makes that kind of claim, I think you ought to have the right to ask whether or not he is telling the truth. As George MacDonald, the famed Scottish minister and author of yesteryear, once said, "Doubts are the messengers of the Living One to rouse the honest. They are the first knock at our door of things that are not yet, but have to be, understood."[6]

Dr. Timothy Paul Jones has discovered MacDonald's words to be true—the hard way. In his fascinating book, *Misquoting Truth*,[7] Dr. Jones reveals that during his first semester at Bible college, he came to experience a serious crisis of faith that shook his belief system to its core.

"It wasn't as if my professors were attacking the Bible," he says. "They weren't. But, with each lecture and reading, my assumptions about the Scriptures—assumptions I'd held since childhood — had crumbled into hopeless fragments."[8]

Rather than shrug his shoulders and walk away, he decided to "rouse the honest" within him, to ask the hard questions, to find the truth and accept whatever it was — even if it meant disbelief instead of belief.

> I could no longer blindly embrace the Bible as divine truth. I needed to know *why* and *how*. Why did so many elements of Christian faith seem to be borrowed from other religions? . . . And, if no one had possessed a perfect copy of the Greek New Testament for nearly two millennia, how could my New Testament possibly tell me the truth about God?[9]

So he spent many late evenings and weekends digging into the university library, devouring this book of history, that book of theology, this textbook on Greek language, that magazine article on linguistic accuracy, and more. Listen to how he describes what happened next:

> I did the only thing I knew to do.
>
> I kept at it.
>
> I kept reading everything I could find, searching for some distant, glistening of truth. And finally, near the end of my second semester of college, the clouds of doubt began to clear — not all of them, and not all at once. But, bit by bit, faith reemerged.
>
> It wasn't the same sort of faith that I had possessed when the semester began. In truth, my faith had grown in the darkness. Now it was far deeper, far richer, and

far better equipped to understand what it means to embrace the Bible as God's Word. After seven months of seeking truth, truth finally found me.[10]

It is interesting to discover who this relentless college student turned out to be. Some years later, Dr. Timothy Paul Jones is one of the most eloquent and accessible of all Christian theologians, a seminary professor, and a best-selling author of several influential books in defense of Christ and the Christian faith. Imagine what our community of believers would have lost had he been unwilling to challenge the core of his being and ask those uncomfortable, life-altering questions about faith!

I am encouraged by these stories of the Woman at the Well, by the apostle Paul, by people like Dr. Timothy Paul Jones, and the like. Why? Because I, too, have often faced doubts in the darkness. I, too, have sometimes paused and said to myself, "Is this really the Christ?" In every instance, in every case, asking that question has always given me the same result, sometimes quickly, sometimes not so quickly.

While those moments of questioning occasionally threatened my belief system, in the end they have always strengthened my faith. That's not because I have somehow stumbled upon all the answers to my questions — oh no! I have questions all the time! Tons of them! But it is because sometimes those questions have been answered, and other times those questions have taught me to say, "I just don't know the answer — yet — but I know the One who holds the answer away from my understanding, and I will trust that he knows what he's doing."

I believe the Woman at the Well eventually got to that place in her life too, but when she first hurried into Sychar and asked,

"Could this be the Christ?" I think she must have also been asking, inwardly, the corollary to that question: What if Jesus really is who he says he is? What does that mean for me?

What If the Answer to the Question Is Yes?

A few years back my husband, Mike, was fortunate enough to interview best-selling and award-winning author Philip Yancey over lunch at a downtown Denver eatery. As you may know, Philip Yancey is one of the great Christian thinkers of our time, and his works and words have had a profound influence on my own life as a follower of Christ.

At any rate, during their chat, the conversation turned to Christianity and why Philip Yancey believed it to be true. Here's what he had to say:

Mike Nappa (MN): Philip, the question we're often asked is this: How do you know that Christianity is true? Why are you a Christian and not some other religion, or no religion at all?

Philip Yancey (PY): Bishop William Temple in England said this phrase. The first time I heard it, it struck me as strange. I had to think about it a lot: "In God is no un-Christlikeness at all."

What that means, in common English, is if you want to know what God is like, look at Jesus. Look at

Jesus. If you read just the Old Testament that we've talked about, you will see failure after failure after failure. Nobody's content. God's irritable, unhappy, disappointed. The Israelites are irritable, unhappy, disappointed, and almost wiped off the face of the earth. When the Old Testament ends, David's tromped on by Syria and Persia and Babylon, and the next few years, they're tromped on by Greece and by Rome. It's a disaster. And in the midst of all that, the prophets have said, "Yeah, but something's going to change. Something's going to change."

Now nobody predicted what actually did happen. None of the people of the time recognized it, and that's God became a human being. . . . Now, we know that Jesus was not kind of God's last-second idea. He had it in mind from the foundation of the world, as the Epistles tell us. But why did Jesus come? What difference does he make?

Well, if you're just stuck with the God who is revealed in the Old Testament, compared to Jesus, you're missing a lot — missing an awful lot. And God in Jesus found a way to bridge the gap. He showed us what God is like — in God is no un-Christlikeness at all — and he showed us what we should be like. And so, the cross is an appropriate emblem because it's these two lines that come together and never again meet. That's what Jesus does, and Jesus really doesn't allow us the option of considering him just one of many. He's pretty clear. "I am the One. I am the One sent by God to bring the world to God."

MN: In most of your books, you seem to work hard to challenge us believers to face the truth about a relationship with Jesus. Why do you suppose we need that kind of challenge?

PY: Well, the reason I emphasize that, I suppose, is that I was brought up in a church that told you *not* to think. And they would say, "Don't question. Just believe." And the things I was told to just believe I found out later were lies, a lot of them. "Just believe that black people are inferior to white people." And they'd point to a verse in Genesis that would tell the curse of Canaan and all that, and I, for a time, I threw out the whole [Christian] thing because I realized, "Man, this is a bunch of nonsense."

Later I realized, "Well, yeah, that's true. It is a bunch of nonsense, but *somewhere in there is a core of truth that is the most important thing in the world.* What is that core of truth?" So my process ever since has been to "reclaim those words." They were spoiled, they were distorted, and often they were the opposite [of truth]. . . . So I think my process as the pilgrim is just to go back and reclaim those words and find *truth* that I could claim for myself, and then for anybody else who happened to follow along.[11]

For Philip Yancey the answer to the question, "Could this be the Christ?" is shown in logical, consistent ways — and that's a good thing. While faith is certainly essential to the Christian life, that faith need not be ignorant. Simple, rational reasoning can often dispel any worries of eternal significance.

Still, when the Woman at the Well needed to weigh the evidence in answer to her question, I think it's important to recognize that it was a personal, emotional factor that seemed to hold the greatest sway.

"Come, see a man who told me everything I ever did," she said.

Look closely at the implications behind those eleven words. For her the greatest proof of Jesus' deity was not that he spoke with authority on theological issues, not that he had disciples willing to give up everything to serve him and study under him, not that he was a respected religious leader, not even that he had boldly claimed to be the Christ. What resounded most loudly within her logic system was that Jesus knew her, knew the details of her mundane life as though they were his own. "Come, see a man who told me everything I ever did," she said. *He knows me,* she must have thought. *Knows me like no one has ever known me before.*

"Could this be the Christ?"

I have to tell you, I've had more than my share of people tell me I'm foolish for persevering in the Christian life. The news media, our popular culture, even a few well-meaning friends. They all think I'm wasting my life in dedication to what they see as a flawed, unintelligent, historically inaccurate, and even subversive religion. "Jesus is not God," they say. "He is a malleable historical figure who represents what some people want to be God, and someone whose legacy has been manipulated into a deified story. But Christianity is mostly just a myth based on a few scattered historical facts. Why waste your life believing anything different?" So they shake their heads at my stubbornness of faith and walk away twirling their fingers next to their temples, hopeful that I am at least one of the harmless crazies out there.

What they don't understand is that there is more to my belief than simple logic or factual reasoning. Yes, logic and intelligence and rational study are certainly worthwhile pursuits in matters of faith, and they certainly can strengthen our lives of belief. But no amount of human wisdom will ever be enough to truly justify complete faith in anything — not in science, not in religion, not in social codes, not in legal issues, not in philosophies, nor in whatever else demands an element of trust coupled with understanding.

So the question comes to me, "Could this be the Christ?" and I immediately answer, "Yes," fully confident that my answer is correct. But how can I be so sure? How can I be so certain that Christ is who he said he was? Let me explain it this way.

Let's imagine for a moment that I show you a picture of my husband and say, "This is Mike. He's my husband of more than twenty years."

If you are a skeptic, you may say to me, "Hmm. I see a man in this picture, but how can I know that he is really your husband? I don't see you in the picture with him. What if this is just your idealized image of a husband? What if you have simply longed for a husband, and so you have adopted this romanticized image as your husband and created an elaborate fiction of a marriage, and even doctored up some document to look like a marriage license? I've seen other marriage licenses, and I've never once seen your husband's name on any of them. How can I believe that your marriage license is not a forgery, or mistaken at best? What if your husband doesn't really exist? I talked to a different man yesterday, and he said he was your husband. What if someone merely convinced you that he was your husband, but he's really just an identity thief? Or a con man? Or maybe part of a husband conspiracy designed to keep women in bondage to husbands? Really, how can you believe this is anything more than a picture of a man — and one that's probably been touched up and doctored to look like something better than the real thing anyway? No, I don't believe in your husband. The weight of the evidence is too heavily stacked against it, the 'shadow of a doubt' is much too large, and really, all I have to go on is your word that he is your husband. Sorry, but I'm not buying it, and I don't think you should believe in that husband garbage, either."

Now, honestly, if you are me, will any of those arguments convince you that Mike is not my husband? For that matter, is there anything anyone can say that will convince you that my husband either doesn't exist or is merely a forgery to feed my emotional instability and inherent desire for a husband? Of course not! You could lay out logarithms or theorems, you could present supposed archaeological evidence, you could bring a dozen witnesses who tell me my husband is just one of the great conspiracies of history, but you will never succeed in convincing me that Mike isn't my husband. Why?

Because I *know* him, intimately, deeply. I know his morning rhythms, I know his sense of humor, I know his chocolate-brown eyes and comforting smile. I know the sound of his whisper in the night and the love that hides in his laughter. I know the scent of his presence and, to some extent, the intangibility of his soul. I *know* this man, and all your logic and intellectual arguments simply aren't enough to overrule my own experience of a relationship with him.

And better yet, *he knows me*. We are intimates — friends and lovers who have had our souls knitted together over the many days, weeks, months, and years. Were he to disappear from my life at this moment and never appear again, I would still never waver in my belief in him. We know and are known together, and nothing can ever change that in my life.

You see where I'm going with this, don't you?

Just as I *know* Mike, in some indefinable way that is actually deeper and more real than my relationship with my husband, I *know* Jesus Christ. Personally. Intimately. In ways that simply can't be logically described or scientifically tested. And better yet, *he knows me* — just as he knew the Woman at the Well, just as he knows you and your thirsty soul. We are known together, and nothing can ever change that, not in my life, not in yours.

Sometimes people will say to me, "What if it's all a lie? What if Jesus just isn't the answer?" And my response is always the same . . .

What if he is?

What if Jesus is this person he claimed to be? What does that mean, in practical, relevant, nitty-gritty terms for you and me today? After all, if it's true that Jesus is the Son of God, then our lives can never really be the same, can they? My experience tells me this is truth; it can be your experience too.

"Come, see a man who told me everything I ever did. Could this be the Christ?"

A few thousand years ago the Woman at the Well asked that question of her neighbors in Samaria. Now, today, as we near the end of this chapter and the end of this book, I think I will ask the same question of you.

Could this Jesus that you've heard about, that you've read about, that you've thought about . . . could this be the Christ?

And if he is, what does that mean for you, right now, today?

The Scripture indicates that the Samaritans' response to this question was to go check out this so-called Christ for themselves, to scrutinize and analyze the man and his words.

So what are you going to do?

engaging the promise

Many of the Samaritans from that town believed in him because of the woman's testimony, "He told me everything I ever did." So when the Samaritans came to him, they urged him to stay with them, and he stayed two days. And because of his words many more became believers.

They said to the woman, "We no longer believe just because of what you said; now we have heard for ourselves, and we know that this man really is the Savior of the world."

— JOHN 4:39-42

She stood on the edges of the crowd, near the women and children, listening and drinking it all in. The educated men asked the first questions, listening skeptically but respectfully to his answers. Then others took up the conversation. Soon they were all sitting around the well listening to this man, this Jewish stranger, the one they now called Rabbi Jesus, talk about the wonderful and unknowable things of God.

It was a child who sidled up to her at first, a young girl with wide eyes and a look of wonder on her face. "Did he really tell you all about your life? Did he really know about you like he knows these other things about God?"

The woman nodded, eyes mirroring the wonder of the girl's. "He told me everything I ever did."

The young girl smiled and nodded, and skipped away. Soon she was whispering in her mother's ear. And then the mother was at her side. "Is it true?" the mother asked.

"He told me everything I ever did," the woman repeated. The mother raised her eyebrows in suspicion. She apparently knew something of the past. The woman nodded solemnly. "Everything."

For the next few hours several people — women, children, and even a few men — came and asked the same question. And every time the woman gave the same answer.

Finally the sun lay low in the western sky and the children began to be restless and hungry. Someone said, "Come to my home for dinner so that we can hear more."

Another said, "Stay the night with us so that we can hear more."

Several others said, "Please, we've so much to learn. Please stay with us, teach us of yourself and of the Messiah of God."

And this was the miracle: He stayed.

Two days later the city of Sychar was an altered place, and the woman knew that she, too, had been changed from the inside out. Jesus, the one-time stranger, was finally continuing his interrupted journey to Galilee, but his time with the Samaritans had changed everything. Yes, there were many questions still left to be answered and many worries and concerns left in life. But now there was a tangible hope, a real-live reason to live, and a wealth *of Jesus' teaching from which to draw lessons of eternity and of the individual moments that lead up to it.*

As the people stood on the edge of the town watching Jesus and his disciples walk away, they also began to gather where the woman stood. These people had, only days before, been willing to associate with her only out of necessity; now they came of their own free will and treated her as an equal, with respect.

"We no longer believe just because of what you said," they said to her when Christ was finally out of sight. "Now we have heard for ourselves, and we know that this man really is the Savior of the world." She treasured those words like the precious jewels they were, because she also had finally reached the same conclusion about that stranger she'd first met at the well.

And for the first time in a long memory, her thirsty soul felt satisfied.

I am sometimes annoyed with Jesus' disciples, and in this instance I am particularly frustrated with the apostle John.

It was John who first recorded the encounter of Jesus with the woman beside Jacob's well outside the city of Sychar. It was he who painstakingly reconstructed the conversation between these two. Truth is, he was not physically present when Jesus first spoke to this Woman at the Well, and so he must have copied down the contents of their conversation at a later time, drawing from the memories of Christ and the woman. It is likely that he unearthed the details of their meeting during the two days that Jesus and his disciples stayed in Sychar while on this journey. And I think John did a wonderful job of capturing for history the scene and details and words of that first encounter.

What really irks me, though, is that John *was* physically present with Jesus in Sychar for the next two days — yet he neglected to take down any of the words that Jesus spoke during that time!

I can only imagine the force of truth behind those words of Jesus to the Samaritans living in Sychar. After all, when a brief forty-eight hours had passed, the Scriptures seem to indicate that just about everyone in Sychar had come to believe — beyond a shadow of doubt — that Jesus was indeed the physical fulfillment of Old Testament prophecy that was thousands of years old.

"Now we have heard for ourselves," they said, "and we know that this man really is the Savior of the world."

What could he have possibly said that was so convincing? What mere words could Jesus speak that would be so decisively accepted by a full community of people — people who were Samaritans no less, and who would have been inherently distrustful of any Jew, let alone a Jewish rabbi?

I suppose I will never know in this lifetime (thanks *a lot*, John — you lazy bum!), but I am still grateful for what the apostle did record, and for the Woman at the Well he remembered in his writing. After all, because of her, I have learned a few very important things about life, about faith, and about the thirst-quenching promise found in the person that the Samaritans once called Savior of the world. As we near the end of this book, I hope you will let me share those lessons with you now.

The Promise Is Possible

Recently I read a fascinating essay by the prominent children's author E. B. White. Before his children's career, E. B. — or Andy, as he was known to his friends — earned his stripes as a columnist for the famed *New Yorker* magazine during the 1920s and 1930s. Upon the success of his children's novels like *Charlotte's Web* and *Stuart Little*, he eventually left New York City to take up residence in Maine, where he lived and wrote until his death in 1985.

At any rate, just a few years after World War II, White was invited back to "The City" to write an experiential essay for *Holiday* magazine detailing his impressions and explorations of postwar life in the Big Apple. His essay was published and was shortly after released in book form under the title *Here Is New York*.

Reading E. B. White's prose is a delight unto itself, but also catching a glimpse of his insight into the possibilities and realities of urban life is simply beguiling. Near the end of *Here Is New York*, however, I actually did a double take. Reading, as I do, from a post-9/11 mentality, I still feel with an unfair freshness the pain and unexpected horror of the terrorist attack on the World Trade Center in late 2001. Imagine my surprise, then, when I read these words of E. B. White — words that were written some five decades previously, all the way back in 1948:

The subtlest change in New York is something people
don't speak much about but that is in everyone's mind.
The city, for the first time, is destructible. A single flight
of planes no bigger than a wedge of geese can quickly

end this island fantasy, burn the towers, crumble the bridges, turn the underground passages into lethal chambers, cremate millions. The intimation of mortality is part of New York now: in the sound of jets overhead, in the black headlines of the latest edition. . . .

Of all targets, New York has a certain clear priority. In the mind of whatever perverted dreamer might loose the lightning, New York must hold a steady, irresistible charm.[1]

With an almost prophetic vision, E. B. White predicted both the terrorist motivation and method — and the devastating after-effects of what an attack of planes "no bigger than a wedge of geese" might inflict on the city and on our nation. Something that most people would have considered unthinkable, White saw as both possible and probable. His was a dark but accurate promise of heartache yet to come.

The Samaritans of Jesus' time had already seen the dark promises of history come to pass, in the subjugation of their people first to the Babylonians and later to the Romans. For the Samaritan woman beside Jacob's well, the promised vision for her community was the exact opposite of E. B. White's vision for New York City — but no less true. White's near-prophetic statements alluded to disaster; but the truly prophetic messages of the Old Testament promised hope and understanding.

"I know that Messiah is coming," the woman had said earlier in her conversation with Jesus, and at the time it seemed a distant promise, a fuzzy hope, both for her and for the other Samaritans living in the town of Sychar. Then, moments later, she was rushing through her hometown shouting, "Could this be the

Christ?" Could this promise actually be *possible*? she seemed to be asking. Could it be happening right here, right now, in our lives today? And that curious possibility of God's promised Messiah was enough to draw both the hearts and bodies of the Samaritan community straight to Jesus.

Realize, my friend, that this claim of Christhood was not something that anyone would take lightly at that time or at that place! The mantle of Messiah carried with it not only invisible, spiritual assumptions of divinity but also very real, tangible, earthly consequences. A fourth-century Samaritan text called the *Memar Marquah* documented the traditions and beliefs of earlier centuries of Samaritan people, referring to the promised Messiah as one they called the "Restorer." Listen to the expectations these people had of this God-sent Savior: "The Restorer will come in peace and reveal the truth and will purify the world and establish the heads of the people as they once were."[2] Those are some pretty big shoes to fill!

Theologians also remind us of the weight of the mantle of Christ. "When this expected deliverer would appear," says Lawrence O. Richards in his comments on John 4, "God's hidden plans and purposes were to be unveiled."[3] John Walvoord and Roy Zuck add, "The Samaritans expected a coming messianic leader . . . a Moses-like figure who would solve all their problems."[4]

Based on Moses' words in Deuteronomy 18:18-19, the Samaritans believed that this promised Messiah was expected to be like Moses, to be, at the very least, of Moses' stature and authority, and to speak the very words of God himself. In addition he was to be the one who would one day restore both the people and the Samaritans' temple on Mount Gerizim.[5]

So you see, claiming to be the Messiah — and believing someone's claim of Christhood — was not something to be taken lightly!

How in the world could this inconspicuous rabbi, just passing through Samaria, sitting thirsty beside a well, be that world-purifying, truth-revealing, Moses-like, promised Messiah? Who would realistically believe something as preposterous as that?

And yet the promise was *possible* — and the fact that it was possible was enough to drive the crowds out from Sychar and into the presence of Jesus, just to find out if it could be true.

The Promise Requires Patience

I find three things to be interesting about the way this particular historical record in John 4 ends. First, the people of Sychar obviously wanted to meet the promised Messiah. After all, when the woman came racing through town shouting, "Come, see a man who told me everything I ever did. Could this be the Christ?" there's no indication that anyone hesitated. Just the opposite, actually. It appears as though they, like the woman, dropped whatever it was that they were doing and immediately came rushing out to Jacob's well to meet this would-be deity (see John 4:29-30).

Second, unlike so many of his other stops across the Judean countryside during the years of his ministry, Jesus did no physical miracle for any of these people. He healed no blind man, he raised no child from the dead, he fed no families with a miraculous multiplication of bread, he didn't even change water into wine. The closest thing he did to a miracle was to tell a stranger that he knew something of her past, something that (honestly) was not a secret in her little community at Sychar. He could have easily had that information passed on to him with a bit of investigatory preparation by his disciples. Yet for many in that Samaritan village, that personal knowledge appeared to be proof enough.

The apostle John reported, "Many of the Samaritans from that town believed in him because of the woman's testimony, 'He told me everything I ever did.'"[6] As Walvoord and Zuck comment, "The testimony of the woman [at the well] . . . was effective. That Jesus knows what is in a person and that he has comprehensive knowledge of one's life is an indication of his deity."[7]

Still, it's the third thing that most intrigues me about this encounter: It is the patience of the promise displayed in Jesus that I cannot seem to ignore. "So when the Samaritans came to him, they urged him to stay with them, and he stayed two days," the Scripture reports. Apparently the woman's testimony and the initial meeting with Jesus himself still wasn't quite enough for some in the crowd. "Stay here awhile," they urged. "Tell us more. Help us understand."

What surprises me is not that they asked Jesus to stay — that seems only natural. What strikes me here is that *he honored their request*, delaying his journey two full days in order to answer their questions and provide assurance to their doubtful minds.

Remember why Jesus was passing through this region to begin with? Listen to what the apostle John reported earlier: "The Pharisees heard that Jesus was gaining and baptizing more disciples than John. . . . When the Lord learned of this, he left Judea and went back once more to Galilee."[8]

One commentator explains Jesus' actions here in this way: "When Jesus learned that his growing number of followers was arousing the attention of the Pharisees, he left the region, probably to avoid a confrontation with them."[9]

In short it appears that Jesus was, temporarily at least, running away from a fight with the dominant religious leaders of his time. Remember that this village in Samaria was not terribly far from where Jesus had come. What if some spy from the Pharisees had followed him here? What if word got back to the Pharisees that Jesus was over in Sychar claiming to be divine? Or, perhaps even worse in that time and culture, what if the news got around that Jesus, this so-called Son of God, was now tainting himself and his reputation by associating with the despised Samaritan population, women included?

New Testament scholar Craig Keener emphasizes the stigma of that kind of association, saying, "For Jesus to lodge there [in Samaria], eating Samaritan food and teaching Samaritans would be roughly equivalent to defying segregation in the United States during the 1950s or apartheid in South Africa in the 1980s — shocking, extremely difficult, somewhat dangerous."[10] With full knowledge of these social, religious, and possibly legal ramifications, do you know what happened next?

Jesus stuck around.

Do not underestimate the power and risk of the patience Christ showed to this Samaritan community. Not only did he place himself under the scrutiny and dubious protection of his Samaritan hosts, he also subjected his disciples to the same treatment and stigma. Why would he do that? Well, as Keener so aptly puts it, "The Jesus of the gospels is more concerned with people than with custom."[11]

Or perhaps you'll let me describe this moment in another way. Back at the beginning of this book, I led you through a scene in Antoine de Saint-Exupéry's treasured book, *The Little Prince*. I think it's fitting, then, that in this last chapter we revisit another moment in that profound children's story.

Near the end of this book, the Little Prince is traveling alone through the earth when he happens upon a wild fox. As their conversation progresses, the fox says,

> "To me, you are still nothing more than a little boy who is just like a hundred thousand other little boys. And I have no need of you. . . . But if you tame me, then we shall need each other. To me, you will be unique in all the world. . . . Please — tame me!"[12]

The Little Prince is filled with compassion for the fox, and so he asks, "What must I do, to tame you?"

> "You must be very patient," replied the fox. "First you will sit down at a little distance from me — like that — in the grass. I shall look at you out of the corner of my eye, and you will say nothing . . . but you will sit a little closer to me every day . . ."

So the Little Prince tamed the fox.[13]

Do you know what I see when I glimpse the crowd of Samaritans rushing out of Sychar to discover Jesus standing beside the ancient well? I see Antoine de Saint-Exupéry's little fox, living alone, yet longing to be tamed.

Do you know what I hear when they call out to Jesus and

urge him to stay with them? I hear that little fox crying into Christ's eternal soul, "Please — tame me!"

Again, it doesn't surprise me that they would beg for him to stay. They are *all* thirsty after all, and he alone holds the living water to quench the longing for eternity within their hearts.

What fills me with wonder is that *Jesus stayed.*

That he interrupted everything to take the time to "tame" this lost community of foxes.

That the promised Messiah was also the patient Christ, willing to stick around for two extra days simply because a sin-soaked, grimy-faced Samaritan asked him to do it.

The Promise Is a Person

As those two extra days come to a close, so also does John's recorded history of that encounter of Jesus with the Woman at the Well. "Because of his [Jesus'] words many more [Samaritans] became believers," John reported. "They said to the woman, 'We no longer believe just because of what you said; now we have heard for ourselves, and we know that this man really is the Savior of the world.'"[14]

As I mentioned earlier, it irks me just a little bit that, after watching Jesus interact with the Samaritan people for two full days, John neglected to record any other conversations Christ had with others from the town of Sychar. (You can see I have a hard time getting over things!) And, as I mentioned earlier, Scripture gives no indication that Jesus performed any physical miracle at all during his stay in this region. The only thing he offered as proof of his divinity was his words, his thoughts, his wisdom, his conversation.

And that was enough. "We have heard for ourselves," the Samaritans declared, "and we know . . ."

The intellectual person within me longs to pore over exactly what those Samaritans heard from the lips of Christ over those two days, would love to dissect every word and phrase in an exercise of scholarly discovery. But were I to do that, I might miss what the Woman at the Well and the rest of her Samaritan cohorts were able to quickly discern:

The promise of God is, first and foremost, a person. The person of Jesus, the lover of our existence, the single personality from whom our souls can receive living water that will well up within us as eternal life. As Walvoord and Zuck so eloquently perceived, "True faith moves to its own experience and confrontation with Jesus."[15]

And there's where the Woman at the Well found herself, where the Samaritan villagers found themselves, and where you and I must find ourselves today. It is helpful to study science and theology and sociology and history and language and more. But it is only in an individual, personal, intimate "confrontation with Jesus" that the promise of the Messiah and the satisfaction of his living water can truly be found. In the end it's all about him, about that Person who first made a divine appointment with a thirsty woman at a well in the lowly town of Sychar in Samaria.

This is a hard life, my friend. You know that already. The Woman at the Well knew that. Even the Samaritans from the village of Sychar knew that. But the true reason we all need a Messiah, a Savior of the world, is not so much because of *what* that Messiah can *do* for us (though that is certainly important) but because of *who* the true Messiah *is* to us.

Notice that when Jesus finally walked away from Sychar, he left that town in much the same state as it had been when he arrived. He hadn't, as previously expected, solved all the problems of Samaritan society. He hadn't overthrown the Roman occupiers. He hadn't rebuilt the temple on Mount Gerizim. He hadn't even draw up blueprints or organized a building committee to study the environmental impact of messianic prophesy fulfillment. But all those things didn't matter in the end. What mattered was that Jesus is who he said he was — the Christ, the promised Messiah, the Son of God, the Savior of the world.

You see, when all is said and done, it is irrelevant whether or not Jesus fulfills our preconceived notions and theological interpretations of divinity and prophecy. What matters is the *person*, that he is the embodiment of the *promise*, and that we can live in intimate relationship with him. We, like children who simply haven't learned all there is to know yet, can trust him to be and do all that he really is — regardless of how that plays out in our individual life circumstances.

Put more simply: He is God. We are not. And if we would embrace the promise of God, we must first learn to trust the embrace of the Promise of God — Jesus himself.

This is difficult, not only because as citizens of the twenty-first century we have inherited skepticism and hypocrisy as part of the legacy of our world culture. But also because we, like the Woman at the Well, are so often people who have fallen short, who have been bruised by sin, scarred and demoralized by our own actions, handicapped by our own emotional shortcomings, and distrustful of our own potential to be redeemed.

This world hurts, and trusting Christ is certainly no guarantee of a painless existence — especially since the harm we experience can often be traced to negative consequences of our own selfish, unhealthy actions. Yet into this life of difficulty and self-inflected sinfulness, the Promise has come — and he intends to stay.

"God finds us worthy of his concern in spite of our ruin," says Lawrence Richards, reflecting on the impact of the life of the Woman at the Well. "God values us enough to actively seek us, to welcome us to intimacy, and to rejoice in our worship."[16]

I am nearing the end of this book now and find myself overwhelmed by this last moment. What can I say here to bring home the message of this chapter, of this book, of the Scripture we've spent these last days and hours poring over together? How can I communicate one last time the power of this encounter between Jesus and the Woman at the Well that's described in John 4? What can I say to let you close this book with the encouragement that God loves you, a thirsty woman, with the same intensity and care he displayed thousands of years ago beside Jacob's well near Sychar?

I think perhaps I will leave you with one last story, a true one, about Hannah Jones.

In 1996, Hannah had been born in Romania and immediately abandoned to an orphanage. She was adopted by an American couple and moved to the United States. A few years later they also abandoned this bright, spunky child. So, by the time she was only seven years old, Hannah had already been orphaned twice.

In 2003, Timothy and Rayann Jones stepped in as Hannah's foster parents. Six months later they adopted her, making Hannah a permanent part of their family and home. Given her life experience to that point, it will come as no surprise to you that Hannah occasionally had some difficulties in her new family and with trusting the sincerity of this latest in a long string of parental figures.

"So will you always be my daddy now?" she asked her new father not long after her adoption was finalized.

"Yes," Timothy responded immediately. "For always."

As a way to emphasize his dedication and love for his new daughter, Timothy began a morning ritual that was, at first, a little uncomfortable for both. Before he left for work each day, he stopped by Hannah's room to give her a hug.

I'll let him describe the rest:

[On the first morning,] I knelt beside the bed and slid my arm around the child's shoulders. As I drew Hannah close to me her body stiffened and her eyes flashed open. She looked wildly around the room and then stared into my face. Thus far in her brief life, she had lived with three different sets of parents in a half-dozen homes in two countries. At this moment she did not seem to be certain where she was or which parent it was that now held her.

"It's okay," I whispered. "It's your daddy. This is your new home. Remember? It's me."

Hannah nodded mutely, but her body stayed stiff and her eyes remained wide. Ever so gradually, she began to relax. Finally, she snuggled close to me and fell asleep in my arms . . .

In this way, a ritual began. Each morning I slipped into Hannah's room to hold her for a few moments.

Each morning she awoke with a burst of confusion and fear. Then, slowly, she drew close to me and rested.

Our routine continued for nearly three months. Then, one Saturday morning in August, something happened.

I knelt beside Hannah's bed, gently pulled her body toward me, and her eyes did not open. At first, a burst of sheer terror chilled my stomach. *Was she okay?*

Then it happened.

Hannah settled herself into my arms and murmured softly, "I love you, Daddy." With this she returned to sleep. . . . In place of the terror there was trust. She knew my touch so well that she had settled into my embrace without even opening her eyes to make certain it was me.

She had learned to trust my hands even when she could not see my face.[17]

It's interesting to me that soul thirst knows no age limit. Like the Woman at the Well, like you, and like me, little Hannah felt the dryness of the soul that comes with exposure to the arid plains of this life. The lonely moments in a stranger's house. The hidden fear that manifests itself in an abandoned life. The self-inflicted blame and punishment of other's failures. The hurtful attitudes and actions used as protective emotional and physical armor against inward despair. Were she able to understand it at the time, I think that seven-year-old Hannah might easily have whispered the same words we encountered at the beginning of this book.

"I am about to die of thirst," Antoine de Saint-Exupéry's

pilot said in the desert.

Yet just when Hannah might have been tempted to give up, to give in to the harsh, cracked, waterless environment that threatened to take over her life, she learned to trust yet one more time. And in that trust she found a father who would love her "for always."

Like Hannah, I walk through this desert of life with a companion who has promised to love me "for always." And in my life's desert, it is often not I who reach out to grasp him but Jesus who comes in to embrace me. He holds me tightly as we cross the sun-scarred troubles of my life, across my frequent failures and mistakes, over the dunes of my selfishness and sinfulness, beyond the broken rubble of my plane-wrecked relationships and foolish decisions. He never tires of holding me up, of taking me just one step farther.

And slowly, ever so slowly, I am learning to recognize his touch and the deep tenor of his voice. "It's okay," he whispers to me. "We're not home yet. Remember? It's me."

Slowly, ever so slowly, I am learning to close my eyes, to let his breathing overcome my own instinct to hyperventilate, to let his living water begin to soak the red, dry soil within me.

Slowly, every so slowly, I am learning from the example of friends like you, dear reader, and those who have gone before, like the Woman at the Well. I am beginning to understand that Jesus is who he said he was, that he loves me, and that he can be trusted. No matter what.

I said earlier in this book that thirst does not kill; absence of water does that. Thirst drives us to remember, to live, and to seek life-giving water. And so now I am grateful for the thirst, painful though it may be, because it was thirst that first drove me to Jesus and later demanded that I write this book.

I am grateful for the thirst because through it I found a river of living water in the person, in the promise, in a personal friendship with Jesus, who is the Christ.

May you and I always know that kind of thirst of the soul — and the familiar satisfaction of having it quenched by Christ's Holy Spirit each and every day of our lives.

Amen.

come to the water

Let anyone who is thirsty come to me and drink.

— JOHN 7:37, NCV

Thank you, my friend, for going on this journey to Jacob's well with me. It has changed me, and I hope, in some small way, it has been helpful for you as well. After all the stories and all the time we've shared together, I'd be remiss if I ended this book any other way than to allow you an opportunity to add one more story to it — your story.

Perhaps as you read through the pages here, God's Spirit began speaking to you, calling you to him. Perhaps you've never given your life fully to Jesus Christ. Perhaps it's finally time for you to respond, to make your own meeting with Jesus beside the well of your life.

The message is simple. All of us — you included — have done wrong. The Bible calls that sin and reports that the penalty of sin is eternal death. That's the bad news.

The good news is that God sent his Son, Jesus Christ, to pay the penalty of sin. Jesus gave his life, suffering and dying by crucifixion, to pay that penalty. And then, to show that he was more powerful than sin and death, Jesus rose from the dead, coming back to life with an offer of life to all who would believe. He offers life to you.

Listen to how the Bible describes this:

For everyone has sinned; we all fall short of God's glorious standard. (Romans 3:23, NLT)

The wages of sin is death, but the free gift of God is eternal life through Christ Jesus our Lord. (Romans 6:23, NLT)

If you confess with your mouth that Jesus is Lord and believe in your heart that God raised him from the dead, you will be saved. For it is by believing in your heart that you are made right with God, and it is by confessing with your mouth that you are saved. As the Scriptures tell us, "Anyone who trusts in him will never be disgraced." (Romans 10:9-11, NLT)

And so now we are back to you. Would you like to experience the forgiveness and renewed life that God, your Father, offers you? To begin to sip on the living water that wells up to eternal life within the soul? If so, it's only a prayer away.

Open your heart to Jesus. Pray to him. Ask him to forgive the failings of your past, to erase the penalty of your sin. Ask him to fill you with his Holy Spirit, to enable you to follow him for the rest of your life, to formally adopt you into the family of God.

Why not do it now?

After you have prayed, please contact a church near you and let someone know about it. Tell the folks there that you have just given your life to Jesus and would like help to learn more about following him.

And if you think of it, drop me an e-mail to let me know about your new story too. I'd love to hear from you. You can e-mail me through the "contact us" page at www.Nappaland .com.

I look forward to hearing from you soon.

— Amy Nappa

for group discussion or personal reflection

A Note from the Author

I always find I get more out of a book if I talk about it with a few friends. So here's a great excuse to get together with three or four girlfriends, eat yummy snacks, and talk. Use the questions here to prompt discussion about what you've learned, what's challenged you, what you agree or disagree with, or what you want to do differently in the days ahead. I do recommend that you make an agreement ahead of time that what's shared in these discussions stays there — and doesn't become the topic of gossip. (After all, you don't want a friend to feel cast away as the Woman at the Well did!)

Or, if you're not really into sharing deep thoughts with others, you can use the questions here to reflect on during your own personal time. Jot down your musings. Refer to them later.

Either way, I hope Jesus will meet you during these times and that you'll find refreshment for the thirst in your soul.

— *Amy Nappa*

Introduction: A Little Prince

1. Can you remember a time when you felt incredible physical thirst — as the Little Prince did wandering in the desert? Talk about that time.
2. What do you remember of the feeling of taking a drink of water after that time of thirst?
3. What about spiritual thirst? When have you felt spiritually thirsty? Compare that thirst to physical thirst. How are these thirsts the same? Different?

One: Waiting

4. Where do you usually think of Jesus waiting for you — perhaps on the couch during a quiet moment of the evening? At the breakfast table when the day is starting? Where would you *expect* to find him in your life?
5. When was a time you met God in an unexpected place? Share that story.
6. God cherishes you. Think about that for a moment. What does that mean to you? Do you believe it or not?

How could believing this statement change something in the way you live?

Two: Experiencing the Unexpected

7. What's the most surprising thing *you've* done lately? Has life gotten into a rut? What could you do that would be totally unexpected? (It should be something fun!)
8. How has God surprised you lately? What happened? What did you do? What are your "normal" expectations of God?
9. This chapter says, "God's surprises are good, but they are not always comfortable." Do you agree or disagree? Explain your answer.
10. What's an uncomfortable situation you've had that allowed you to draw closer to Jesus? To learn something new about him? To learn something new about yourself?

Three: Teasing the Mystery

11. What's your favorite mystery? Nancy Drew? Sherlock Holmes? Or a fast-paced thriller mystery? What do you like (or not like) about mysteries?
12. What in your own life feels like a mystery?
13. Have you seen God work through a mystery already? How can what you've seen God do in your past help you trust him with your current situations?
14. Do you believe that "it all turns out well"? Why or why not?

Four: Facing the Hidden Reality

15. What's a memory you have of trying to hide something as a child? Are you able to laugh about it now? What lesson did you learn at the time?

16. Only share this out loud if you're truly comfortable. But even if you don't share it out loud, think about it. What is a secret you're still hiding right now? How does it feel to know that God already knows this secret?

17. What does it mean to you to be hidden in God's heart?

18. Read Romans 8:35,37-39 aloud. What does this passage mean to you? Do you believe it? Does it show in your life that you believe it?

Five: Speaking the Truth

19. Are you the kind of friend who speaks the truth (even if it might hurt a little) or one who prefers to leave things alone? Do you think your approach is better? Why or why not?

20. Have you ever had a sin exposed in an embarrassing way? If so, what happened? How did you grow from this experience?

21. Have you accepted the truth about Jesus Christ? Or are you still pushing it away?

22. What is a truth that's been hard for you to speak aloud to someone? What would give you the courage to speak the truth?

Six: Removing the Distractions

23. What physical flaw are you best at hiding? Why do you think we, as women, are so interested in hiding our physical flaws? What would happen if we were open with others and ourselves about our true appearances?

24. What about the internal flaws? How are you at hiding those? What would happen if we came out from behind the curtain with those internal imperfections? Which is more frightening for you — to let others see your physical flaws or your internal flaws? Explain why.

25. Pull away the curtain right now. In a moment of silent conversation with Jesus, let him see your heart. Be open as you talk about what you see and what you know Jesus sees. How does it feel to be honest with him?

Seven: Revealing the Hope

26. If, as the lyrics of the song imply, hope could call out to you, what would it say?

27. Consider this statement from chapter 7 again: "And hope, once realized, is worth all the hardship and heartache that came from holding fast to its promise of something better." Do you believe this is true? Why or why not?

28. What hope are you holding to right now, and what hardship or heartache are you going through as you hold fast to that hope?

29. What are the "easy hopes" you're relying on now? Are

you willing to exchange those for "difficult hope"? What would it take for you to make that step?

Eight: Processing the Revelation

30. Talk about a time you were stuck in an awkward silence. Remember that feeling for a few moments, and imagine yourself in the shoes of the Woman at the Well, experiencing that same feeling. What's it like?

31. When have you been *comforted* by a time of silence? Can you embrace silence as a moment of rest? What would it take for you to get away for one whole hour of silence this week and just listen? Can you make it happen?

32. Have you ever run away from a situation and then learned a surprising lesson in the process? If so, share about that time.

33. Do you believe Jesus is pursuing you? What would happen to your perspective in life, your relationship with Jesus, if you took that truth to heart?

Nine: Examining the Christ

34. If you were the Woman at the Well, who would you have run to for that second opinion? Who are those people who can help you dig into what you're learning and verify what's true and what's not? You need these friends! If you don't have them, find them!

35. What are your questions — hard questions of faith or just questions about stuff you don't "get"? List them

in your journal. It's okay to be honest!

36. What can you learn about yourself from your list of questions?

37. Why do you think so many Christians are afraid to ask questions, to admit that they even *have* questions?

38. What are you going to do with your questions?

Ten: Engaging the Promise

39. Take a few minutes to reflect. What's the message from the chapter you want to remember most? Discuss that or write it down.

40. When are you most thirsty? How has your relationship with Jesus quenched that thirst?

41. What can you learn from the thirsty moments?

42. How can you avoid becoming so thirsty? We're told to drink a lot of water to keep our bodies hydrated. How can you stay spiritually hydrated?

For Further Reflection

To dig more deeply into the spiritual themes explored in *Thirsty*, get a Bible and check out the following Scripture passages:

- Psalm 42:1-2
- Isaiah 55:1
- Revelation 22:17
- Psalm 63:1
- Psalm 107:9,33
- Isaiah 41:17
- John 6:35

notes

Introduction: *A Little Prince*

1. Antoine de Saint-Exupéry, *The Little Prince*, trans. Katherine Woods (New York: Harcourt, 1943), 76–79.

One: *Waiting*

1. John Cox, from an interview by Mike Nappa / Nappaland Communications Inc., May 1997. Transcript © 1997 Nappaland Communications Inc. Reprinted and adapted by permission. All rights reserved.
2. Craig A. Evans, *The Bible Knowledge Background Commentary: John, Hebrews–Revelation* (Colorado Springs, CO: Victor, 2005), 57.
3. Evans, 56–57; Craig S. Keener, *The IVP Bible Background Commentary: New Testament* (Downers Grove, IL: InterVarsity, 1993), 272.
4. Evans, 57.

5. R. Kent Hughes, *1001 Great Stories and Quotes* (Wheaton, IL: Tyndale, 1998), 260.

Two: Experiencing the Unexpected

1. Adapted from "Random Acts," an unpublished article by Larry Shallenberger. Copyright © 2005 Larry Shallenberger. All rights reserved. Reprinted by permission. (Contact the author at www.LarryShallenberger.com.)
2. Of course, two can play at that game. Maybe next time I go on a trip with some of my girlfriends, I'll come home and surprise him with a Wonder Woman tattoo or something!
3. Andrew Snaden, *When God Met a Girl* (Colorado Springs, CO: LifeJourney, 2007), 92–93.
4. Ken Wakefield, in discussion with the author, June 2007. (Ken Wakefield is Amy Nappa's uncle.)

Three: Teasing the Mystery

1. "It's a Mystery," *Shakespeare in Love,* DVD, directed by John Madden (New York: Miramax, 1998). Transcribed by the author.
2. Ralph Gower, *The New Manners and Customs of the Bible* (Chicago: Moody, 1987), 250.
3. Chip Heath and Dan Heath, *Made to Stick* (New York: Random House, 2007), 84.
4. Heath, 84–85.
5. Heath, 85.
6. Colossians 2:2.
7. Colossians 4:3.
8. 1 Corinthians 13:12, NCV.
9. Job 42:3.

Four: Facing the Hidden Reality

1. Jody Brolsma, in discussion with the author, July 2007. (Jody Brolsma is Amy Nappa's sister.)
2. C. S. Lewis, *The Last Battle* (New York: Collier, 1956, 1970), 136–141.
3. Lewis, 143–148.
4. Romans 8:35,37-39.
5. John L. Cooper and Korey Cooper, "Hey You, I Love Your Soul" (Photon Music/BMI, 1998). From the album *Hey You, I Love Your Soul* (ForeFront Records, 1998).
6. Cooper and Cooper
7. Linda Carlson Johnson, *Mother Teresa: Protector of the Sick* (Woodbridge, CT: Blackbirch Press, 1991), 55–56.

Five: Speaking the Truth

1. Max Lucado, *Just Like Jesus* (Nashville: Word, 1998), 112.
2. Notes for John 4:18, *The Archaeological Study Bible, New International Version* (Grand Rapids, MI: Zondervan, 2005), 1726.
3. Lawrence O. Richards, *Bible Teacher's Commentary* (Colorado Springs, CO: Victor, 1987, 2004), 718.
4. Ron Mehl, *The Cure for a Troubled Heart* (Sisters, OR: Multnomah, 1996), 20–25.
5. dc Talk and the Voice of the Martyrs, *Jesus Freaks* (Tulsa, OK: Albury Publishing, 1999), 144.
6. Winston Churchill, as quoted by John Fischer, "There It Is: A Daily Devotional," *PurposeDrivenLife*, June 5, 2006, http://www.purposedrivenlife.com/devarchive.aspx?ARCHIVEID=1803 (accessed July 14, 2007).
7. Candace Lombardi, "CBS Resizes Couric in Promo Pic,"

CNET *News.com*, August 30, 2006, http://www.news
.com/8301-10784_3-6110890-7.html (accessed July 13, 2007).

8. Zahea Nappa, in discussion with the author, July 2007.
(Zahea Nappa is Amy Nappa's mother-in-law.)

Six: Removing the Distractions

1. Lawrence O. Richards, *New Testament Life and Times*
(Colorado Springs, CO: Victor, 1994, 2002), 227.

2. Cuesta College, "Recognizing Propaganda Techniques and
Errors of Faulty Logic," Cuesta College Academic Support,
http://www.academic.cuesta.edu/acasupp/AS/404.htm
(accessed July 22, 2007).

3. Cuesta College.

4. Nora Ephron, *I Feel Bad About My Neck* (New York: Alfred
A. Knopf, 2007), 5.

5. Ephron, 4.

6. Eric Gjovaag, "What's the Wizard's Name?" *The Wonderful
Wizard of Oz Website*, http://www.thewizardofoz.info/faq05
.html#22 (accessed July 22, 2007).

7. "The Wizard Revealed," *The Wizard of Oz*, DVD, directed
by Victor Fleming (1939; Burbank, CA: Warner Home
Video, 1999).

8. Donna Lamb, "Samaritan Woman," *She Shall Be Called
Woman, Volume II*, ed. Sheila Jones and Linda Brumley
(Woburn, MA: Discipleship Publications International,
1995), 59.

9. "Fish Impressions" and "Jellyfish," *Finding Nemo*, DVD,
directed by John Lasseter (2003, Disney/Pixar, 2003).

10. Acts 26:2-20, NCV.

11. Rick Lawrence, *Jesus-Centered Youth Ministry* (Loveland, CO: Group, 2007), 164.

Seven: Revealing the Hope

1. Ambrose Bierce, *The Devil's Dictionary* (New York: Dover Publications, 1911, 1993), s.v. "hope."

2. C. S. Lewis, *Mere Christianity* (New York: Macmillan, 1952), 118.

3. Christine Dente, "With All My Heart" (Mighty Grey Music/ Lil' Yella House Music/Dayspring Music/BMI, 2001). From the album *6.1* (Rocketown Records, 2001).

4. Philip Matyszak, *Ancient Rome on Five Denarii a Day* (New York: Thames & Hudson, 2007), 22.

5. Matyszak, 59.

6. Matyszak, 61.

7. Rick Hoganson, "Miracle Baby Arrives at Hands and Feet Project in Haiti," Hoganson Media Relations press release, July 26, 2007.

8. Gien Karssen, *Her Name Is Woman* (Colorado Springs, CO: NavPress, 1975), back cover.

9. Karssen, 177.

10. Kathleen McGowan, "The Pleasure Paradox," *Psychology Today* 31, no. 1 (January/February 2005): 52–53.

11. "Visiting the Family," *Million Dollar Baby*, DVD, directed by Clint Eastwood (2004; Burbank, CA: Warner Home Video, 2005).

12. Wanda Luttrell, *Timeless Needs, Eternal Hope* (Colorado Springs, CO: LifeJourney, 2007), 52.

13. Luttrell, 49.

Eight: Processing the Revelation

1. Craig S. Keener, *IVP Bible Background Commentary: New Testament* (Downers Grove, IL: InterVarsity, 1993), 274.

2. Mother Teresa, as quoted by Mike Nappa in *The Courage to Be Christian* (West Monroe, LA: Howard Publishing Co., 2001), 140.

3. Keener, *IVP Bible Background Commentary*, 274. Also Lawrence O. Richards, *New Testament Life and Times* (Colorado Springs, CO: Victor, 1994, 2002), 226.

4. Lawrence O. Richards, *Bible Teacher's Commentary* (Colorado Springs, CO: Victor, 1987, 2004), 718.

5. Terry Esau, *Surprise Me* (Colorado Springs, CO: NavPress, 2005), 49.

6. Margaret Wise Brown, *The Runaway Bunny* (New York: HarperCollins, 1942, 1970).

Nine: Examining the Christ

1. John F. Walvoord and Roy B. Zuck, *The Bible Knowledge Commentary: New Testament* (Colorado Springs, CO: Victor, 1983), 287.

2. Mike Nappa, in discussion with the author, July 2007. (Mike Nappa is Amy Nappa's husband.)

3. See Matthew 26:63-64; John 4:26; John 6:35; John 8:23; John 11:25; John 14:6; John 14:9.

4. Mike Nappa, in discussion with the author, July 2007.

5. Associated Press, "Bush Stands Too Tall for Wary Boy," *Phoenix Gazette*, March 12, 1991.

6. Harry Verploegh, *3000 Quotations from the Writings of George MacDonald* (Grand Rapids, MI: Revell, 1996), 73.

7. And by the way, if you are looking for a book that discusses

the hard questions about the accuracy and relevance of the Bible, Dr. Jones' book *Misquoting Truth* is among the most readable — and most honest — books I've seen on that subject. It's highly recommended!

8. Timothy Paul Jones, *Misquoting Truth* (Downers Grove, IL: InterVarsity, 2007), 18.

9. Jones, 19.

10. Jones, 20.

11. Philip Yancey, from an interview by Mike Nappa / Nappaland Communications Inc., June 1999. Transcript © 1999 Nappaland Communications Inc. Reprinted and adapted by permission. All rights reserved.

Ten: Engaging the Promise

1. E. B. White, *Here Is New York* (New York: The Little Bookroom, 1949, 1999), 54.

2. *Memar Marquah* 2:33, 70, 180. As quoted in *The Archaeological Study Bible, New International Version* (Grand Rapids, MI: Zondervan, 2005), 1727.

3. Lawrence O. Richards, *Expository Dictionary of Bible Words* (Grand Rapids, MI: Regency Reference Library / Zondervan, 1985), 162–163.

4. John F. Walvoord and Roy B. Zuck, *Bible Knowledge Commentary: New Testament* (Colorado Springs, CO: Victor, 1983), 286.

5. *The Archaeological Study Bible*, 1727.

6. John 4:39.

7. Walvoord and Zuck, *The Bible Knowledge Commentary: New Testament*, 287.

8. John 4:1,3.

9. *The Quest Study Bible, New International Version* (Grand Rapids, MI: Zondervan, 1994), 1470.

10. Craig S. Keener, *The IVP Bible Background Commentary: New Testament* (Downers Grove, IL: InterVarsity, 1993), 274.

11. Keener.

12. Antoine de Saint-Exupéry, *The Little Prince*, trans. Katherine Woods (New York: Harcourt, 1943), 68–70.

13. de Saint-Exupéry, 70–72.

14. John 4:41-42.

15. Walvoord and Zuck, *The Bible Knowledge Commentary: New Testament*, 288.

16. Lawrence O. Richards, *Bible Teacher's Commentary* (Colorado Springs, CO: Victor, 1987, 2004), 718.

17. Timothy Paul Jones, *Hullabaloo* (Colorado Springs, CO: LifeJourney, 2007), 24–26, 156–158, 168.

bibliography

The Archaeological Study Bible, New International Version. Grand Rapids, MI: Zondervan, 2005.

Evans, Craig A. *The Bible Knowledge Background Commentary: John, Hebrews–Revelation.* Colorado Springs, CO: Victor, 2005.

Gower, Ralph. *The New Manners and Customs of the Bible.* Chicago: Moody, 1987.

The Holy Bible, New Century Version. Nashville: Word, 1987, 1988, 1991.

Holy Bible, New International Version. Grand Rapids, MI: Zondervan, 1973, 1978, 1984.

Holy Bible, New Living Translation. Wheaton, IL: Tyndale, 1996.

Keener, Craig S. *The IVP Bible Background Commentary: New Testament.* Downers Grove, IL: InterVarsity, 1993.

Matyszak, Philip. *Ancient Rome on Five Denarii a Day.* New York: Thames & Hudson, 2007.

New American Standard Bible, The Open Bible Edition. Nashville: Nelson, 1960, 1962, 1963, 1968, 1971, 1972, 1973, 1975, 1977.

Richards, Lawrence O. *Bible Teacher's Commentary*. Colorado Springs, CO: Victor, 1987, 2004.

———. *New Testament Life and Times*. Colorado Springs, CO: Victor, 2002.

Vamosh, Miriam Feinberg. *Daily Life at the Time of Jesus*. Herzlia, Israel: Palphot Ltd., n.d.

Walvoord, John F. and Roy B. Zuck. *The Bible Knowledge Commentary: New Testament*. Colorado Springs, CO: Victor, 1983.

about the author

AMY NAPPA is a best-selling and award-winning author of many books, including *A Heart Like His* and *A Woman's Touch*. More than a million copies of Amy's books are in print, and her work has been translated into several languages, including Korean, Spanish, and Dutch. Additionally, Amy is the cofounder and associate publisher of *www.Nappaland.com* — "The Free E-Magazine for Families" — and she is a popular speaker to women's groups and educational ministry gatherings nationwide.

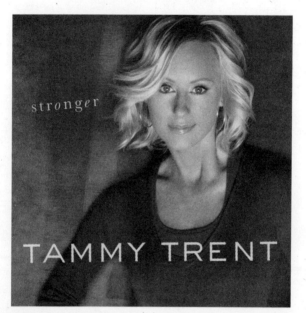